DATE DUE

INTERNATIONAL
RELATIONS
IN THE
BIPOLAR
WORLD

STUDIES IN POLITICAL SCIENCE

CONSULTING EDITOR | INIS L. CLAUDE, JR.

INTERNATIONAL RELATIONS IN THE BIPOLAR WORLD

PETER J. FLIESS

UNIVERSITY OF MASSACHUSETTS

RANDOM HOUSE

NEW YORK

First Printing

Copyright © 1968 by Random House, Inc.
All rights reserved under International and Pan-
American Copyright Conventions. Published in
New York by Random House, Inc., and simul-
taneously in Toronto, Canada, by Random
House of Canada Limited
Library of Congress Catalog Card Number:
68–16367
Manufactured in the United States of America
by The Colonial Press Inc., Clinton, Mass.
Design by Christina Hager

TO MY MOTHER

PREFACE

The course of world politics since the end of the Second World War has followed sufficiently novel paths to warrant a reexamination of the familiar assumptions of foreign policy. The novelty consists, in essence, of a fundamental redistribution of international power. As a result of the vast disparity in military and economic resources, which has emerged in the wake of the war, the power and influence of the major nations has become differentiated to a degree that contrasts sharply with the traditional concert of roughly equal major powers. Of even greater consequence has been the displacement of the former multiplicity by two superpowers, the United States and the Soviet Union, whose possession of unmatched means of destruction has put them in a class by themselves and made them the only plausible guardians of international order. The conventional theoretical framework of international law and international relations, applicable to the political relations between a sizable number of roughly equal states, has, therefore, been frequently irrelevant to the problems that have arisen since 1945. The wide gap in physical power makes it imperative to differentiate clearly in both theory and practice between the United

States and the Soviet Union, on the one hand, and the rest of the world, on the other, and to appraise the effects of the de facto differences that have developed in the quality of international powers.

This book will attempt to clarify the nature of bipolarity and to demonstrate its peculiarities. It will endeavor to describe and explain trends and events, and to examine the adequacy of current policies and ideas, showing how men act under bipolar conditions and why they act as they do. Inasmuch as this study is concerned with power relations— the stuff of international politics—no attempt will be made to judge the standard of values of the main contestants in terms of transcendental norms, to analyze the spiritual malady of our age, or to search for a panacea that might cure it. If the task at hand requires us to emphasize the element of necessity inherent in bipolarism as an important determinant of political and strategic conduct, this is not to advocate a fatalistic surrender to impersonal forces, but to suggest the limits of what is possible and prudent. It is therefore essential to bring into focus the various facets of the irreducible dilemma that confronts the world today.

A word should be added to justify what may appear as an undue emphasis on the peculiarities of bipolar politics. It certainly is not our intention to imply that old political problems do not recur or, when they do, that they cannot often be dealt with in previously proven ways. It should suffice here to make the obvious point that, although basic trends have changed and the needs growing out of the present political constellation are new, human nature continues to provide an element of stability. Moreover, it scarcely needs mentioning that the new alignment of powers is not the only political development of note. There have been other developments that have complicated the issues and altered the logic and rigidity of bipolarity. Among them are anticolonialism, equalitarianism, the decline of liberty, the growing trend toward totalitarianism, the advance of democracy, the move toward socialism. Another complicating factor is the geographic extension of world politics to the limits of the globe and perhaps even into outer space. The difficulties of analysis are further aggravated by the impact of the unprecedented technological and scientific advances of our age, which have tended to obscure the political problem. But it is the political setting with which this study is concerned. The choice of that focus is not to suggest that politics are separable from the contemporary state of technology or that they do not have to be related today to nuclear strategy. It is merely for the didactic purpose of making the political issues stand out more clearly that they will receive special emphasis over the larger social-technological complex.

I am deeply indebted to Professor Inis L. Claude, Jr., the editor of this series, whose constructive criticisms were of immeasurable value. I also wish to express my gratitude to Charles D. Lieber, who encouraged me to follow up an earlier work on bipolar politics in the Peloponnesian War with a study of contemporary bipolarism. Miss Anne Dyer Murphy provided patient and considerate editorial guidance, and Miss Sybil Elman was responsible for reducing inconsistencies and stylistic flaws. The efficient secretarial services of Miss Josephine C. Scurria were of invaluable help in the preparation of the manuscript.

P.J.F.

CONTENTS

CHAPTER FIVE
THE SUPERPOWERS AND THEIR CLIENTELE   100

CHAPTER SIX
THE NONALIGNED   135

CHAPTER SEVEN
IDEOLOGY, POWER, AND LAW   161

CHAPTER EIGHT
CONCLUSION   196

**INTERNATIONAL
RELATIONS
IN THE
BIPOLAR
WORLD**

CHAPTER ONE

BIPOLARITY: MYTH OR REALITY?

BIPOLARITY DEFINED

The term "bipolarity" has entered into discussions of international relations only since the end of the Second World War. Much to the dismay of a generation that had only recently been engaged in a war to end all wars, it signified the continuation of tension and violence in world politics. The victors' utopian vision of a brave new world of enduring peace had failed to materialize. Instead, mankind was awakened to the challenges arising from a new and, it seemed, unprecedented constellation of powers. The passing of the roles of world leaders from European to peripheral powers alone signaled a revolutionary change. Even more revolutionary was the unprecedented concentration of effective international power during the course of the war and the concurrent reduction in the number of leading powers. The former system of world politics dominated by a sizable number of delicately balanced major powers has given way to a power dualism, in which the ultimate responsibility for the maintenance of international order falls to only two superpowers. Through their unmatched thermonuclear as well as economic and industrial power, the "Big Two" have, in a dual sense,

3

become the leading forces in the world. Their lead in arms technology has given them the exclusive possession of total destructive power and thus has made them the ultimate determinants of human destiny. At the same time, their economic and industrial strength has made others dependent on them for the military and economic aid needed to build or maintain modern societies. Such dependence has given the superpowers a unique influence and has made them the directors of the course of world politics. International stability, consequently, depends chiefly on the balance between these powers, and few issues of more than purely local significance remain free of their intercession.

BIPOLARISM AS A SYSTEM

Contrary to what one might expect, the polarization of international power has failed to produce a clear, simple pattern. Relations between the superpowers and the rest of the world are far from being a one-way street. Notwithstanding the overwhelming military strength of the superpowers, other powers have, from the outset, resisted attempts to do their bidding. Such resistance has become more frequent and determined with the passage of time. Through trial and error, the superpowers have had to learn that it is not possible to manipulate international society from a command position but that persuasion and maneuver remain the proper methods of international intercourse. The perseverance of traditional forms raises two fundamental questions concerning the bipolar balance. First, can it be contended, in the absence of a straight-line relationship, that the functions of the superpowers in world politics are so unique and of such consequence as to necessitate a distinction between the traditional multilateral and the new bipolar balance of power? Second, can it be argued, in the face of the intractability of other powers, that the controlling position of the superpowers is essentially unimpaired and likely to remain so, that is, that manifestations of polycentrism, however vocal, are of no actual significance for the main course of world politics?

A glance at the record of international relations during the first two postwar decades clearly shows the profound effect that the emergence of two superpowers has had on world politics. The impact of the redistribution of power will be more closely examined in detail in the following chapters and summarized in the Conclusion. However, two important developments can be mentioned. One is a marked simplification of international politics as compared with the situation under the traditional multipolar system. There has, for example, been a manifest tendency for international crises to be settled bilaterally by the Big Two instead of by general international conferences. A case in point is the civil war in Laos in the early 1960's. Instead of leaving matters in the hands of the contending Laotian factions or convening an international conference, a cease-fire was negotiated by the American President and the Soviet representative. Similarly, the 1962 Cuban missile crisis was resolved through bilateral negotiations between the American and Russian leaders with scant attention to the wishes of the Cuban government or other powers. The response of the two powers to the recurrent unrest in Cyprus is another example. In the Middle East the Arab-Israeli war of 1967 has clearly shown that the only hope for stabilizing relations between the Arab states and Israel rests on a settlement that is jointly supported by the United States and the Soviet Union.

Moreover, the respect that the superpowers have generally shown for the autonomy of other powers since the mid-1950's has not prevented them from interposing in disputes between other states, even in the absence of alliance obligations. The self-involvement of American diplomacy in the Kashmir dispute between India and Pakistan is a case in point.[1] A more vivid expression of the unique and ambitious role seized by the superpowers is a statement by the American Secretary of State, Dean Rusk, in which he proposed that American military action go beyond the country's treaty commitments to maintain the status quo.[2] Disclaiming any intention to establish a Pax Americana, he based his position on the important part played by the United States in supporting the United Nations in its peace-saving efforts.

The second development is the increased stability and predictability of international relations as compared with the past. While the possibility of predicting the actions of the great powers was enhanced from the outset for those who understood the workings of the new balance, the formative years of bipolarism were marked by a tenuous stability. During the first decade after the Second World War, the superpowers displayed an inordinate sensitivity to each other's moves, leaving international stability in a position of extraordinary precariousness. Since then, hazards have been greatly reduced by the nuclear stalemate between the Big Two, and rationality and control in international relations have become possible. As the Big Two became accustomed to the new situation their international conduct showed an increasing tendency toward sobriety and rationality. That tendency has been further strengthened by a widening area of common interests, which has resulted from new international conditions. No longer does the staffing of leading positions in the United Nations automatically find the United States and the Soviet Union bitterly opposing each other. In the summer of 1966, when U Thant made known his unwillingness to serve another term as Secretary-General, the United States found the Soviet Union prepared to cooperate in attempts to persuade him to remain. The wide area of agreement that exists between the two powers was accentuated by President Johnson's appeal to the Soviet Union to join the United States in an effort to secure world peace and, more particularly, to limit nuclear diffusion.[3] The stabilization of the nuclear status quo has been the main area of common interest. What delayed a formal agreement was the anticipated reaction of third powers. However, a concern for the sensibilities of others did not remain an obstacle when a formula was worked out that accommodated the interests of both leading powers.

When all this has been acknowledged, we are still faced with the problem whether the changes in the operation of world politics are so basic as to compel us to look upon bipolarism as a distinctive "balance of power system." The matter is of some practical importance for a systematic exploration of the rules inherent in the reordering of international forces. Questions of this type are never easy to answer. In this case, the difficulty is compounded by the lack of general agreement in theorizing about the "balance of power" concept. Much uncertainty and confusion has surrounded both components of the concept. There is no need, in this context, to analyze the constituents of power or to attempt to decide whether the term should be used in a narrow military sense or in a broader one. In the bipolar context, "power" denotes both the ability to make others do one's bidding by whatever means, and the capacity to resist the pressure of others to do that bidding.

The meaning of "balance" is more difficult to ascertain. The various senses in which the term has been used have been the subject of a recent, perceptive analysis.[4] Here, bipolarism will be treated as a balance of power *system* since, as is the case in other balance systems, autonomous power units stand in a more or less close reciprocal relationship without being controlled by a single superior authority.[5] Such a relationship rests on a set of rules ensuring order and stability, and whose infraction would have highly unsettling effects upon the system. Like any other system, the bipolar balance of power represents an order protected by its guardians against disturbances of the basic power relations that are essential to it. What distinguishes it from other systems is an approximate equilibrium of the unique destructive capabilities of two powers, which lesser sovereignties can neither reduce nor augment by withholding or giving their support. The new balance, to be sure, has not wholly invalidated the rules and politics that applied to the traditional balance. In many respects, traditional and bipolar systems still coexist. There remains room to maneuver in accordance with the traditional rules within each bloc and among the noncommitted countries and even, at times, in the relations between the Big Two. But in the long run, bipolar politics overshadow the more diversified relations of the lesser powers, which find it difficult, if not impossible, to resist sustained pressures of the superpowers. In particular, matters of prime importance, such as the avoidance of war, are dealt with in terms of the exigencies of the bipolar balance.

The existence of a system and its distinctiveness can best be observed by contrasting the basic trends and forces at work with the operation of the traditional system. Perhaps the most striking difference is the purpose pursued by the powers on whose support the so-called balances rest. There was substantial agreement among the great powers of the traditional order that preserving a multiplicity of independent states was of paramount importance. Although in theory the multistate system was to be secured by maintaining an approximate balance among the major powers, the aim of the leading powers was more often directed toward unbalancing than toward equilibrating power. The difficulty was perhaps inherent in the existence of a plurality of states. Encompassing many autonomous and frequently unaligned units, the traditional system did not normally present two more or less equal sides. Moreover, the concept of equilibrium had two serious practical drawbacks: the impossibility of measuring power with enough precision to estimate the presence of an approximate equilibrium; and the threat of international instability in the face of precariously balanced powers. It was, therefore, only natural for its members to aim at a preponderance of power over any actual or would-be aggressor to ensure, if the worst came, his defeat, but at least to deter him from carrying out his plans. Since the role of aggressor would not consistently fall to any one power but would more likely be shifting, the system required an uncommitted balancer as guardian, ever-ready to shift its power so as to ensure a preponderance against any troublemaker. For centuries that part was played by Great Britain with admirable efficacy. The system worked as well as it did because Great Britain happened to be more interested in maintaining international pluralism than in seizing world domination.

In the bipolar world, the aims and purposes of the

guardians lie in different directions. Their chief concern is to avoid all-out war without surrendering supremacy to the opponent. The pursuit of that goal implies the balancing rather than the unbalancing of power. In fact, we can now properly speak of a "balance" system in the literal sense. Equilibrium is not only a possibility, but is conceptually implied in bipolarism and is a practical necessity. Many of the former difficulties have been reduced to the simple formula of maintaining and stabilizing the equilibrium between the two blocs. It may seem a curious paradox that balance of power problems should be so simplified at a time when technological developments have created complications appearing incapable of solution. The implications of man's two-pronged advance into the microcosm of nuclear physics and the macrocosm of outer space cannot as yet be fully grasped. And yet the dazzling heights attained by science have relieved the political world of the need to evaluate precisely the various degrees of power at the disposal of both sides. Although the possibility that a disequilibrium may arise at any time cannot be dismissed, unless there is a unilateral technological breakthrough neither side can, with any confidence, expect to destroy the opponent's retaliatory force. Prudence demands that they rest their practical policies on the assumption of roughly equal military strength.

The course is then clearly charted for both superpowers. Their survival as collectivities with some measure of independence forces them to push relentlessly ahead in science and technology, less to destroy the balance than to prevent the opponent from acquiring superior power and attaining world domination. Their apparent striving for preponderance, which they know they are not likely to attain in the intense and costly nuclear missile and space race, is actually aimed at perpetuating the equilibrium of power. It is also becoming increasingly obvious that world domination holds small allurement for either power, since rule over a universal rubble could hardly be an enticing prospect. Actually, both appear more concerned with survival than with the increase and use of power as an end in it-

self. They therefore have little choice but to guard the
present system zealously, with equilibrium as its indispensable condition.

Beneath the clear logic of bipolar strategy, there are
ambiguities and contradictory tendencies. In some respects
the bipolar balance is especially precarious. The fact that
each of the superpowers is only one step removed from
world domination constitutes a constant temptation and
thus tends to create a state of chronic insecurity. However,
the unstabilizing tendencies are outbalanced by the military equilibrium. While preponderance of power may have
been the best insurance of stability under the conventional
conditions, it would always have disastrous consequences
in a bipolar balance, and especially under present-day
technological conditions. There is much evidence to suggest
that the superpowers have fully appraised these facts and
that the preservation of equilibrium has increasingly become the conscious goal of their policy. Such developments, comforting as they are, are no basis for complacency. Trouble spots persist in various parts of the world.
It is far from certain that a *modus vivendi* has been found
in relation to Berlin. And there is reason to fear that the
wars in Vietnam and in the Middle East harbor the potential for a military clash between the Big Two. It must
always be borne in mind that sobriety in international relations, the widening area of common interest, and the
desire to coexist do not imply the end of competition and
animosity.

A final question that must be raised is whether a *global*
balance of power system is at all possible. It is often said
that, despite the political diversity characterizing the European balance of power, the old system had developed and
worked within the context of a homogeneous society of
Western Christian nations united by a common spiritual
and moral bond. The present bipolar system, which is
global in scope, can claim no such unity. Yet one may
wonder whether a power system transcending the orbit
of one single civilization is inconceivable, provided its
members understand how it works and abide, for whatever reasons, by its rules. Although the present worldwide

system does not rest on the common cultural traditions of its members, certainly common interests may provide a sufficiently firm basis to ensure compliance with its rules. A passionate concern with technological progress and the extension of science into the social realm has gripped all parts of the globe. Along with the development of science, there has emerged a universal language that is neither Latin, French, English, nor Russian but is the means of communication of the new international elite, the scientists. Common political experiences have been generated by hegemonial power structures which prevail in the alliance systems on both sides of the Iron Curtain. However, what most unites humanity today is an unprecedented sense of common destiny. A universal fear of impending doom created by the staggering innovations in armaments technology has alerted people everywhere to the likelihood that a nuclear war may be the end not only of enemy populations but also of themselves and possibly of humanity as a whole. In a world divided as it is by traditions and ideologies, a strong desire to avoid a nuclear holocaust provides a sufficiently solid foundation for a community of interests that is worldwide in scope and transcends the former parochialism.

BIPOLARISM AND PLURALISM

A point that must be considered in a discussion of the contemporary bipolar world is the effect of increasing pluralistic tendencies upon the functions of the Big Two, whose power is limited not only by the balance between them but by outside forces. The peoples of the earth have remained strongly attached to the concept of state sovereignty, and nationalism continues to be the most potent ideology. The popular emotions evoked by the image of "nation" largely explain the recalcitrance of third powers to comply with the wishes of the Big Two. Perhaps the chief anomaly disturbing the conceptual symmetry of bipolarism has been the rise of a large number of new sovereignties since the end of the Second World War. The proliferation of sovereignties has not been without effect in world politics. The influence of the new states has made itself especially felt in the United Nations. As a result of the paralysis of the Security Council, their position of equality in the General Assembly has given them an importance out of proportion to their actual or potential military and economic power. The superpowers have de facto acknowledged the importance of the new states by trying to obtain their friendship.

Assertions of independence by third powers, aligned and unaligned, have appreciably limited the superpowers' freedom to maneuver and have been the source of frequent irritation. Even in the absence of common interests and despite their military weakness, the unaligned nations have succeeded not only in making themselves heard in the councils of the United Nations and elsewhere, but also in extracting aid and support from the superpowers. Their policies have been remarkably independent of the Big Two and at times have even crossed the purposes of either or both of them. The matter will be reviewed more fully in a later chapter.

The chief restraint imposed upon the superpowers has been the relations with their allies, which have been marred by frequent and continuing friction. Again, it may suffice briefly to mention the main points, deferring a more detailed analysis until later. During the two decades since the end of the Second World War, both blocs, which had appeared solid in the early postwar years, have become progressively disharmonious. On both sides, the alliance systems have been subject to severe strain. The United States has suffered from an overextension of its alliance systems. It never succeeded in building more than a formal and tenuous unity with its allies in the Middle East and the Far East. But even the most solid alliance, represented in the NATO organization, has been in a condition of serious disarray. The NATO allies have long defied the American nonrecognition of Communist China and the American policy of no-trade with countries of the Communist bloc; they virtually abandoned the United States in the Korean and Vietnamese wars; and they have been seeking military independence to a degree that the United States does not consider desirable. France has continuously refused to fall in step with American policy. With the advent of de Gaulle, Franco-American relations have become increasingly strained. Franco-Russian and Franco-Chinese rapprochements have been followed by French attempts to attenuate NATO and, finally, by France's military withdrawal from the grand alliance. Difficulties have also arisen in the Organization of American States, the American hemispheric defense system. The friendly relations patiently built by American administrations since the days of Franklin D. Roosevelt have yielded to renewed suspicion and resentment with the American intervention in the Dominican Republic in 1965. The United States has made vigorous attempts to mend its alliances, and this has meant frequent deference to its allies' wishes.

Similar cracks can be seen in the Communist orbit. Although less is known about the Soviet camp than about the American camp, it has long been apparent that the power structure of the Soviet bloc is not as monolithic as one may think. The unity of "world communism" has been destroyed by the all but formal withdrawal of China. As early as 1954 China pursued an independent course at the Geneva Conference. Since then, the rift has widened, creating increasingly serious problems for its communist confrere in Moscow. But like the United States, the Soviet Union has suffered some of its greatest embarrassments in Europe. The causes of recurrent tensions between the Soviet Union and its Eastern European allies can be traced partly to nationalism, partly to the emergence of a second communist leader in Asia, and partly to a relaxation of Soviet control after Stalin's death. The first ally to defect was Yugoslavia, which severed ties in 1948. Since then the Warsaw Pact, the Eastern European counterpart to NATO, has shown many signs of weakness. Albania joined the Chinese camp. In East Germany, Poland, and Hungary, resentment of dictation by Moscow led to open revolts. Although these countries have been firmly reintegrated, other members of the Soviet bloc have weakened in their support of the alliance. Rumania and the Baltic states have made no secret of their lack of enthusiasm.

Although they have not withdrawn, they have often refused to cooperate.

Brief mention should be made of another deviation from the bipolar pattern. Transbloc relations, taboo in the early postwar years, have grown in frequency and extent. Since the latter part of the 1950's, trade relations have developed on an appreciable scale between the Eastern bloc countries and the allies of the United States. De Gaulle's rapprochements with the Soviet Union and China preceded France's military withdrawal from NATO. Furthermore, on a visit to the Soviet Union in the summer of 1966, the French President called for a breakup of the polar blocs and the restoration of Europe as a "single whole." [6] Even more remarkable is Japan's attempted rapprochement with the Soviet Union despite old feuds that have long divided the two countries.[7] Significant, too, are West Germany's efforts to expand relations with the Eastern European countries,[8] as is the invitation of the Warsaw Pact countries to the nations of Western Europe, probably issued at the instigation of the Soviet Union, to join them in a "general European conference for the discussion of questions related to insuring security in Europe." [9]

This brief survey clearly shows that world politics are not the exclusive domain of the Big Two. Other forces exist, and their influence cannot be dismissed as inconsequential. However, the question that concerns us here is not whether the superpowers can make their satellites dance to their tunes, but whether the growth of pluralistic tendencies has dislodged the Big Two from their unique position as guardians of the international order or, if they be so inclined, as executioners of the human species. How effectively, it must be asked, has the military and political preponderance of the two powers been challenged?

The development of nuclear weapons by France and China is a major concern; the means of total destruction are no longer the exclusive possession of the United States and the Soviet Union, but are now shared with at least two other nations. So far, the latter's nuclear apparatus are still in their infancy and in no way compare in military effectiveness or political significance with those of the superpowers. But what are the prospects for their bringing their nuclear establishments up to a competitive level without the help of one of the Big Two? Despite the enormous strides made by China in armament technology, as indicated by the explosion of a hydrogen bomb in June 1967, the ability of third powers to attain such a level in the foreseeable future seems a remote prospect. The cost of maintaining an up-to-date force is so staggering as to be beyond the capabilities of any country other than the United States and the Soviet Union. It is equally unlikely that either of the superpowers is prepared to aid third states in building a competitive nuclear force. The Soviet Union is not pleased with the Chinese adventures nor the United States with those of France. On the contrary, both of the leading powers are evidently more interested in preventing nuclear diffusion and, as their agreement of January 1968 shows, they are willing to cooperate in effecting joint control.

There remains, nevertheless, the possibility that the Big Two can be challenged in the political sphere. To break up the bipolar pattern, an appreciable number of allies would have to be pried loose from the Big Two. This could be done only if another force offered advantages, identical or equivalent, to those derived from the present association with the Big Two. The chances that any third power or combination of powers can do this are remote, it is unlikely that third powers will acquire the ability to deter nuclear war or to provide effective protection against territorial encroachments. Not France, China, or any other third power will be able to furnish economic and military aid on a scale comparable to that provided by the Big Two. Moreover, up-to-date military equipment, and in particular nuclear weapons, that many lesser states covet mostly as a status symbol, are obtainable only from the superpowers, even though the latter may be unwilling to provide this kind of aid. As long as the United States and the Soviet Union retain their supremacy in these areas, their controlling position in world affairs remains unimpaired.

The true magnitude of the power of the Big Two is

especially apparent in the relations between the United States and its allies. Although the American alliance system has not been transformed into a tolerably integrated organization of power, as the persistence of lively pluralism indicates, the United States has progressively veered toward unilateralism in its international actions. A number of instances illustrate the extent to which United States foreign policy has liberated itself from external influences. For example, the United States acted swiftly and unilaterally, without consulting either the United Nations or its allies, in filling the power vacuum in Greece and Turkey in 1947, in supporting South Korea with military force after the North Korean attack, and in establishing the Cuban blockade in 1962. The same unilateralism prevails in the American interposition in the Vietnamese War. Attempts to cover up the unilateralism of such actions have not been lacking. In the cases of Greece and Turkey as well as Vietnam, universal doctrines of protecting world peace, checking aggression, or preventing the spread of communism have been proclaimed. The intervention in Korea was subsequently sanctioned by the United Nations, and the Cuban blockade was eventually endorsed by Latin American and the NATO allies. But the relevant point is that third powers neither were consulted nor had the opportunity or ability to oppose or thwart American policy.

The Suez crisis of 1956 is an especially illuminating example of allied relations in the Western camp. The United States made it quite clear that intervention would bring the Soviet Union face to face with American power. Moreover, its insistence on the withdrawal of the Anglo-French forces showed that the United States was not prepared to indulge the extravagances of its Western allies. The decision to accede to the Egyptian *fait accompli* was clearly made by the United States and not by its allies. And the allies' ready compliance proved that the military and, therefore, political capacity of the former world powers—Great Britain and France—had come to depend on American backing.

These examples suggest that a wide gulf exists between the superpowers and the rest of the nations. It can, of course, be argued that in Korea the United States was deserted by most of its allies; that the respective actions of the United States and the Soviet Union in 1956 in Suez and in Hungary seriously hurt the political position of the Big Two and threw their alliances into disarray. However, such setbacks did not shake the central position of the two powers in world affairs or wrest from them the power to make the decisions that will either ensure or threaten the survival of mankind. Their military and economic resources are likely to continue to be unique for some time. Although they may never be able to recapture the degree of control they possessed after the Second World War, the Big Two are now engaged in rebuilding their power positions. While third and even lesser powers are often able to maneuver and exploit big power tensions, they have no independent effectiveness when isolated from the Big Two. Even France and China have implicitly admitted the uniqueness of the United States and the Soviet Union in insisting that nuclear power is the essential mark of a great power in the present-day world.

CHAPTER TWO

THE ORIGINS OF CONTEMPORARY BIPOLARITY

The reaction of Western statesmen to the new problems facing them has been one of exasperation. Accustomed to the ways of multilateral diplomacy, they have shown far less flexibility, ingenuity, and acumen than their more resourceful communist opponents. With considerable bitterness, they have alternately blamed the cynicism of their adversaries and the negligence of their own predecessors for their present difficulties. It may, therefore, be of some interest to examine the circumstances surrounding the development of bipolarism. Even if the new trend was the consequence of the inveterate bungling of shortsighted or ambitious men, it is nevertheless possible that the present condition of the world grew out of a series of historical accidents that could not have been avoided, even if statesmen acted with more circumspection.

THE FIRST WORLD WAR AND ITS AFTERMATH

The early roots of bipolarization can be traced back to the First World War and its aftermath. It was inevitable that the existing territorial order would be profoundly shaken by a war between those powers that had been its guardians for almost 100 years. Although that war did not complete the political destruction, it ushered in a new era of world politics, characterized by the entry of the peripheral powers —the United States, Russia, and Japan. The impact of the new powers upon world politics was no surprise, but its force vastly exceeded the expectations of even astute observers. The new development was further dramatized by the simultaneous decline of the great European powers and the concomitant contraction of the European power system.

The rise of the United States can largely be attributed to the Europeans' desperate need for American assistance to preserve some semblance of the status quo in Europe, the balance of power having been seriously disturbed. But the profound effect of American participation upon the affairs of the Old World was not only due to its great material power; the force of American ideas and values was even more instrumental in making the tired continent receptive to American influence. The optimistic and universalist ideology was in itself attractive enough as a system of thought, but what made it even more appealing was its promise of an imminent better world. Despite their virtues, the new modes of thought did not remain unchallenged for long. A rival source of salvation appeared when the Russians succeeded in rebuilding their political order in accordance with the precepts of Marxian scripture. Inasmuch as the United States was still young and vigorous, it was only natural that a lively competition between the American and the Soviet "experiments," sharpened by the universalist pretensions of their ideologies, should ensue.

The long-range effects of the changes resulting from the war and its aftermath were not immediately apparent, obscured as they were by their frequently paradoxical nature. The increase in the number of sovereignties through the dismemberment of the Hapsburg and Ottoman empires, for example, would scarcely seem to suggest a reduction in numbers of the effective participants in the balance of power system. Therefore, little thought was given to the political consequences of the void left by the dissolution of the prewar empires, and even less was done, in the interest of maintaining the essence of the existing order, to prevent the remaining major powers from extending their control into the vacated space. Curiously enough, the major European states did not benefit from this situation as much as one might expect. The enormous, and rapidly growing, strength of the peripheral nations dwarfed the advantages that the European powers might otherwise have derived from their control over small and underdeveloped areas in Eastern Europe. Moreover, as the balance of power became global in extent, Europe ceased to be the center of gravity. To be sure, the extension of the balance of power had its beginning in the colonial era, which shifted the theaters of war to the far corners of the globe. But it was not until the end of the First World War that the European states were compelled to relinquish their decisive role in world politics in favor of the new extra-European countries. The ascendance of fewer and bigger powers to a dominant position in world politics became more marked during the Second World War. The high concentration of resources and efforts could not fail to reduce political multiplicity further until the formerly diffuse power pattern was displaced by a simple dualism.

THE INTERWAR YEARS

The groundwork for the bipolarization of power was laid with the ambivalent peace settlement following the First World War. The Allies were neither generous enough to offer Germany an acceptable peace nor ruthless enough to reduce the defeated enemy to an economic and political level from which no military comeback was possible. The unstable peace was further weakened by the unwillingness of the Allies to accept the realities of international life, which permitted no pacifist or disarmament schemes. Because of the enormous sacrifices of the war, the victorious Allies permitted themselves to believe in a lasting and advantageous peace. But while they were living under this pleasant delusion, the Germans were relentlessly preparing for a war of revenge, one that would not only restore to them what they felt was rightfully theirs but would also establish them as masters of the world.

During these years the inertia of the victors and the resentments of the vanquished combined to deal the deathblow to the traditional balance of power system. The system was undermined partly by the indifference of some of its more powerful members and partly by the involvement of others in the pursuit of goals that were incompatible with its underlying premises. It was serious enough that Germany, in the 1930's, was ominously headed for war, disregarding the consequences for Western civilization, but it was even more disastrous, and perhaps less justifiable, that the more responsible powers could not muster enough energy to check the disturbance. The Soviet Union's failure to stop German expansionism is the easiest to comprehend; militarily weak, it needed peace and time to build up its defenses. By contrast, the inertia of the Western powers is more difficult to understand and can perhaps be explained only by examining their peculiar ideological blindspots. The faith in the reasonableness of men, who could and would resolve their disputes through rational debate and compromise now that the troublemakers had been overthrown, seemed to have rendered them insensitive to the need of taking timely countermeasures against Germany's aggressive gestations. And the United States' desire to withdraw from world politics through a series of self-denying neutrality laws gave Germany the necessary assurances that it could carry out its aggressive designs with impunity.

A number of other factors can be cited to explain this astonishing lethargy. The peoples of the Allied world were exhausted by the enormous effort that had been required to win the war. Moreover, the balance of power system had been brought into disrepute by Woodrow Wilson's condemnations and it hardly seemed worth preserving by war. In their longing for peace, the Europeans perhaps attributed more effectiveness to the institutional apparatus of the League of Nations and to collective arbitration treaties than was justified. In actuality, the League was severely handicapped by the nonparticipation of some of the major powers. This detracted appreciably from whatever modest contribution collective security, the theoretical principle underlying the League, might have made to international stability. But collective security was dealt its hardest blow by the unwillingness of the member states to live up to their obligations when the League was challenged, placing as they did immediate self-interest above the long-range well-being of the world.

THE SECOND WORLD WAR

The Second World War completed the process of political disintegration. Several phases following each other in quick succession can be distinguished. In its initial phase the war was European in scope. Hitler's strategic and political thinking was still oriented toward the European continent as the focus of world politics. The French and the British also viewed the crusade against Germany in traditional terms after the attack on Poland. However, the dim outlines of new alignments could already be discerned. The time required to produce armaments capable of meeting the challenge presented by the modern equipment of the Germans adversely affected the strategic position of the Western Allies. An enormous initial advantage, therefore, lay with the aggressor as well as with the great and wealthy powers on the periphery, which were not immediately involved in the war.

The war changed, in both scope and method, with the German invasion of the Soviet Union. From the very outset, the war in the East was conceived as a crusade by the Germans; it signified to them a contest between two worlds and two ideologies, a fateful showdown between Europe and Asia. Orders were issued to the armies in the field to conduct the fight with uncompromising harshness and to disregard even the rudimentary forms of civilized warfare.

With the Axis attack upon the United States, the war became global. Germany's plans to establish its "New Order" throughout the world aroused bitter hostility everywhere and produced a united military front against the aggressor. However, political and ideological lines were not clearly drawn. The profound distrust that prevailed in the

Allied camp between the Soviet Union and its Western allies was apparent from the beginning; but only Stalin seemed to have recognized the new trends at an early stage, when he predicted the formation of two world centers followed by a polarization around Moscow and Washington. By contrast, the hostility displayed by Western statesmen to Soviet policies appeared more instinctive than deliberate. The emerging dualism of power became a more conscious factor in the thinking of the Western Allies only with the decline of German power—as Nazism was eliminated from the initially triangular competition between Nazism, communism, and liberalism. The resulting ideological dualism was reinforced by military developments. Whereas the Soviet Union and the United States had, thus far, depended on each other for support, both had attained a high degree of power toward the end of the war and were now capable of singlehandedly finishing the job. The meeting at Yalta, therefore, could take place in an atmosphere of complete equality. Since their belated entry into the war had enabled both powers to build up superior striking forces, the United States and the Soviet Union had suddenly emerged as more or less equal superpowers overshadowing the former world powers.

THE POSTWAR SCHISM

The defeat of Germany created new and, to some extent, unexpected problems. The policies of the United States contributed perhaps more than their fair share to the difficulties of the postwar world and appreciably accelerated the bipolar development. American leaders were by no means neglectful of the magnitude of the political problems that could be expected to follow the termination of the war. In fact, they seem to have given serious thought to postwar planning as soon as war broke out in September 1939. These plans were to ensure that a disaster such as the present war could not recur and therefore required a new international system to displace the traditional pattern. If the balance of power system had not been able to prevent this and past calamities, future world politics could not be left to the results of competitive bargaining but would have to be entrusted to the surveillance and direction of the major powers, who, after the reduction of the congenital aggressor nations, would act in a spirit of cooperation rather than competition.

American leaders realized that the success of an international organization would depend on the presence of certain conditions. The chief requirement was continued cooperation and agreement on the maintenance of peace as the highest good to which all the major powers were dedicated. The effectiveness of a postwar organization as the guarantor of peace clearly presupposed unanimity among world leaders. However, there was much room for doubt that favorable conditions would prevail. Would the Soviet Union not prefer the strengthening of its own power to the building of a peaceful world? There already were unmistakable signs that the Soviet Union was busy filling the power vacuum created by the collapse of Axis satellites in Eastern Europe. And there evidently was considerable uneasiness among American leaders as the Soviet forces advanced into the Balkans. The forebodings of Soviet unilateralism evoked concern that the Soviet Union might become increasingly nationalistic and prefer isolationism to global cooperation. Such fears, however, were assuaged by the tendency to explain the Russian moves as occasioned by security considerations which would be unnecessary with the establishment of the United Nations as an effective security organization.

Although the exasperation of American statesmen with the failures of the past was understandable, their indomitable hostility to the balance of power system was unfortunate. They put their hope in the United Nations as a substitute for the balance of power; it would have been more prudent to look upon the organization as a regulative device.[1] As it was, the burden of maintaining international stability was shifted mainly to the United Nations as a universal organization resting on the principle of sovereign equality for all its members. Spheres of influence were rejected as was the acknowledgment of regionalism in the organizational structure favored by the British and the Russian allies.

American contempt for the balance of power was ultimately to redound to the advantage of the Soviet Union. No counterweight to Soviet power was created in the Balkans. The unconditional surrender of the Axis powers was to create a power vacuum that could not remain unfilled. The readiness of the United States to depart from its traditional isolationism and participate in the occupation of Germany was not enough to hold Soviet power at bay in Eastern Europe. Nor was the United States in a position to deter Soviet ambitions when domestic pressures for immediate postwar demobilization became irresistible. The redistribution of power in Europe in the Soviet Union's favor was further aided by the precipitate termination of military commitments and lend-lease aid to the European allies.

Stalin was less inclined to build on such uncertain prospects. Almost from the outset, he displayed an uncanny alertness to the bipolar trend engendered by the war. His sensitivity to the new developments is not surprising inasmuch as Marxism posits the division of the world into two hostile camps as a matter of historical necessity, leaving no room for genuine cooperation between capitalistic and proletarian powers, except as a temporary expedient. Stalin's ideological commitment alone was sufficient to produce a split; but the rift between the Soviet Union as a continental power and the insular Anglo-Saxon powers was further sharpened by their different approaches to international politics. While the former was preoccupied, to an inordinate degree, with its military security, the latter were mostly concerned with maintaining the status quo, which they tended to revere as a semi-sacred condition. Based on strategic reasons and guided by Marxian ideological precepts, Stalin missed no opportunity, during and after the war, to consolidate Soviet power in Eastern Europe and to create a security sphere by encouraging the establishment of communist governments along the Soviet Union's western frontier. The attainment of these goals would inevitably call for measures that were difficult to square with the principles Soviet leaders had professed and with Russian international obligations. A case in point is the intervention to ensure the victory of communism in Poland in violation of the Yalta agreements. But Stalin, in turn, seemed prepared to respect the interests of the Western powers in what he judged to be their sphere. For example, he refrained from interfering with the British action to squelch the communist uprising in Greece.

Disillusioned with their deceitful ally, Americans became bitterly cynical. Mutual recriminations were soon to supersede protestations of friendship. The main grievances of the United States included violations of agreements or informal understandings concerning the German problem, undue communist pressures in Eastern Europe, and Soviet claims against Turkey and Iran. The Soviet Union responded by accusing the United States of acting unilaterally in relation to Germany, interfering in the affairs of Greece and Turkey, monopolizing atomic secrets, excluding other powers from the occupation of Japan, and supporting the Chinese nationalists. There was, no doubt, some truth in the claims of both sides, but one wonders whether the discord between the former allies can be explained in such simple terms as bad faith, petty rivalry, or traditional distrust between East and West. It may, perhaps, make more sense to seek the causes in the unduly optimistic assumption of the Western Allies that a stable postwar world could be built on the foundation of continued allied unity. The respective ideological commitments of the major powers, East and West, gave ample cause for skepticism, although they did not necessarily preclude cooperation altogether. A more formidable barrier, as shall be shown later, was the gulf created by the bipolar division of power, which could not be bridged even by the best of intentions. It was natural that American statesmen attempted, belatedly, to counteract the dominant position that the Soviet Union had attained in Europe and Asia as a result of the destruction of German military power. But it was just as natural that the Soviet Union was unwilling to let the fruits of victory be wrenched from its grasp.

THE CAUSES OF BIPOLARIZATION

Viewed in terms of political dynamics, perhaps the first step toward the schism was the formation of a united front by a number of great powers pursuing incongruous political goals. The forging of the united Allied front was largely Germany's handiwork in that its outrages and ambitions had created a common interest among the most heterogeneous nations, overshadowing fundamental political discordances. With the German invasion of the Soviet Union both the United States and Great Britain had no choice but to give full support to the victim of the attack. There was good reason to believe that the defeat of the German war machine was possible only if the Soviet forces could be kept in the field, even if this required the diversion of an enormous amount of American material aid from Great Britain to the Soviet Union. To keep the Russians in fighting form and spirit, it appeared necessary to add political and moral support to military support. It was for this reason that President Roosevelt declared in October 1941 that he would refrain from resisting Russian claims in areas, such as Iran, where the interests of the two countries might overlap. Great Britain, too, felt compelled to align with its ally in the East, even if this involved hostilities against a friendly nation, such as Finland.

Although all sides were fully aware of the desperate need for Allied solidarity, signs of disunity were not lacking even in the early phases of the war. Disagreements persisted throughout, particularly with reference to war aims and postwar plans for the organization of peace. Winston Churchill's repeated assurances that communism was no obstacle to building a durable peace were too general and too vague to allay Stalin's apprehensions. At the same time, Churchill's confidence in his ally received a severe blow when he learned of Stalin's plan to incorporate the Baltic states into the Soviet Union as part of the postwar settlement. Stalin's claims were not made any more palatable by his magnanimous offer to support British acquisition of bases in Western Europe. Churchill not only judged the

claims of the Soviet Union incompatible with the principles
set forth in the Atlantic Charter, but he saw no compelling
reason to concede them in advance of a peace conference,
especially since the Soviet Union was in no bargaining position while its survival depended on Anglo-American support.

Allied relations were further strained by the slowness of
the Western powers in opening up a second front in the
West to relieve German pressure against the Soviet Union.
Since September 1941 Stalin had insisted, with unremit-
ting perseverance, on such a relief action. His need no
doubt was urgent. But there was also a psychological aspect
to his persistent remonstrations. The fear never left him
that the Western Allies were not acting in good faith but
were, in fact, anxious to keep the Russo-German war going
until the adversaries would have exhausted each other. Unable or unwilling to see the formidable difficulties of the
operations which he so lightly demanded, he was progressively alarmed by the repeated postponements of the Western attack upon Hitler's "Fortress Europe." In retrospect
there are no indications to support Stalin's suspicions.
Western leaders were far too preoccupied with the formidable problems of war to devote much thought to long-
range political planning. Had Stalin taken the trouble to
study past records of Anglo-Saxon diplomacy, he would,
no doubt, have had to admit the imaginary nature of his
assumptions.

At the root of the intense mutual distrust lay the incon-
gruity of the Allies, which could not be dissipated simply
through protestations of friendship and general promises.
The hostility of the American people to communism was
general and not confined to the propertied classes. It was
reflected in an ill-concealed uneasiness in the face of anti-
German revolts in occupied countries for fear that the
resistance movements might catapult communists into
controlling positions. To be sure, the honest attempts made
by American leaders to overcome their suspicions did much
to alleviate tensions. But their many expressions of sincerity
were never fully appreciated or reciprocated by the Kremlin. In Stalin's mind, a double-cross by the Western Allies

remained a disturbing possibility, and he continued to interpret honest mistakes as perfidy. For example, the erroneous attack by an American airplane upon a Russian unit immediately aroused his suspicion that the United States had switched sides. Under these circumstances, it was impossible to establish genuine cooperation. The most extravagant professions of good intentions could not dispel the misgivings of Eastern and Western Allies about the presence of the other's troops in their domain. American leadership was, nevertheless, ready to accept East-West friendship at face value. But that inclination was quickly eroded by Soviet violations of the most important Yalta agreements within a few weeks after the conference had been concluded. It was at this point that the American President, once again, became distrustful of his ally's ambitions regarding the postwar world.

RESPONSIBILITIES ASSESSED

Historical Forces

Setting aside, for the moment, the question of the desirability of bipolarism, it may be of interest to speculate whether the new power constellation could have been avoided and, if so, to assess the respective responsibility of the various powers. Looking at the circumstances in which the change occurred, what stands out is the rise of the peripheral powers after the First World War and their further growth to gigantic proportions during the Second World War. Viewed in the perspective of time, the revolutionary change in world politics appears less the result of design than of circumstances. It is evident that the Second World War could only be won by the combined manpower of the Soviet Union and the economic resources of the United States. At the height of the war, Russian troops engaged at least two-thirds of the German forces while the United States supplied most of the military equipment for the entire alliance. The predominance of the peripheral powers arose largely from the accidents of geography and world politics, which enabled them to stay out of the war during the first two years. But if impersonal forces favored these powers with a gratuitous respite, they did not permit them to remain aloof indefinitely. Both were closely tied to Europe: the United States by culture rather than by geography; the Soviet Union by geography rather than by culture. However, it was the opportunity to build up their enormous military strength while other major powers were desperately struggling for survival that largely accounted for the postwar bipolarization of power.

The overwhelming show of power by the United States did not, of course, come as a great surprise. Its enormous potential had been impressively displayed during its intervention in the First World War in 1917; it made the difference between victory and defeat for the Allied powers. Since then, the world had time to get used to American influence in world politics. However, the rise of the Soviet Union was a startling development. During the Second World War, Russian strength and influence reached unexpected heights as a result of its deep involvement in the fight against Germany, while the Western Allies were idly standing by. The Allies were not unaware of the political advantages the Russians were accruing by bearing the brunt of the war. Churchill, in particular, was concerned with the relative political standing of Western and Eastern Allies in the crucial postwar situation. He seemed well aware of the political perils resulting from the Soviet Union's heroic performance, which, though impressive by itself, assumed an even more gigantic stature contrasted with Western idleness. "I am deeply conscious," Churchill admitted to Stalin, "of the giant burden borne by the Russian armies and their unequalled contribution to the common cause." [2] The acumen of the British statesman can at least, in part, be explained by his country's impotence in the war against Germany after the fiasco at Dunkirk. The British Empire was already exhausted when the United States was just beginning to unfold its great economic and industrial potential. In the absence of comparable experiences, a similar sensitivity to the political implications of Soviet military successes was not to be expected of the United States. Americans were also less aware of the susceptibility of

European minds to military achievements. But irrespective of their preferences, there was little the Western Allies could do to shorten the period of their involuntary idleness. Preparations for the projected operations in the West required time, and no shortcuts were possible.

A further disturbance was the infusion of ideologies into the conflict, which only served to prolong and embitter the war. The unexpectedly long duration of the war and the ideological zeal with which it was fought were remarkably effective in bringing about the political bankruptcy of Europe, upsetting whatever plans may have preceded its initiation. All of Hitler's plans were based on the confident expectation that even the most powerful enemies could be prostrated through a few swift lightning blows (*Blitzkrieg*) before they had an opportunity to catch their breath. These expectations were foiled by the strong ideological commitment of the belligerent nations. Ideological fervor drove the German nation to fight on beyond capacity. It prevented the Allies, in turn, from negotiating a settlement and inspired them with a determination to fight until the political annihilation of the enemy was complete. In such an atmosphere, there was no reason for reflection on the problems that the political dissolution of the enemy country would inevitably produce. Consequently, instead of restoring the old order or laying the foundations for a new one, the war brought chaos.

Germany's Responsibility

It is against the background of these circumstances that the heroes' and villains' roles in the emergence of the bipolar balance have to be assessed. Our thoughts quite naturally turn first to Germany. Even the greatest passion for objectivity cannot excuse or explain the recklessness of German policy. Any sober statesman must have been aware of the improbability that Germany could hold both the United States and the Soviet Union at bay, and there could never have been any doubt that the failure of Germany's ambitious plans would benefit the Soviet Union by providing the opportunity for enormous expansion. It should have been surmised that Stalinism would replace Hitlerism in postwar Europe. This was all the more likely since Nazi ideology and methods had done an effective job in destroying traditional values and the moral consensus of most of Europe. In the resulting chaos, there were no forces strong enough to stem the forward march of Stalinism.

In its ideological madness, Germany not only destroyed the European order, but created the alliance whose split was eventually to divide the world into two hostile camps. The hatred and contempt generated by Nazi racial doctrines and the atrocities committed by German forces in conquered lands drove heterogeneous nations into a partnership to eliminate one of the most formidable dangers ever to threaten Western civilization. Their single-minded purpose to bring the culprits to justice blinded the Western Allies to the problems posed by a victorious Soviet Union. The task of defeating the neobarbarians was so gigantic as to dwarf the problems arising from the long-range political intentions of Russia. Little thought was given to the disagreements that would inevitably arise between the Allies, once the task at hand was completed. Germany had actually played into Stalin's hands, even before demilitarizing Eastern Europe, by concluding the nonaggression pact in 1939. Had the Soviet Union not been given the opportunity to move its armies westward and build up its war machine, its resistance might have quickly crumbled under the German onslaught in 1941. Evidently, German leaders seriously underestimated the Soviet Union's immense potential.

The Soviet Union's Responsibility

Germany, to be sure, was not singly responsible for the destruction of the traditional order. The Soviet Union too aided the bipolar trend by encouraging Germany, through the nonaggression pact, to carry out its belligerent intentions. It is unlikely that Germany would have started the war when it did if the Hitler-Stalin pact had not guaranteed security on the Russian front. To the Russians, the pact must have appeared a political masterstroke. Overshadowed by Germany's formidable military machine, Stalin, no doubt, was anxious to buy time at any cost. Moreover, in giving Germany the go-ahead signal, he had also ensured the anti-Western nature of the war, which by now appeared unavoidable. From a short-range point of view, the Russian policy cannot be considered anything but realistic if not brilliant. From the long-range point of view, it appears less impressive. Stalin's indulgence in the illusion that he would be able indefinitely to keep the war away from Russian soil was unrealistic. What the effects of a more orthodox Russian policy would have been, is, of course, impossible to estimate. However, one may conjecture that Germany would have been forced to tread cautiously for a while and perhaps even to abandon permanently all plans for a general war. It is, nevertheless, unlikely that a Russo-German showdown could have been avoided indefinitely and, when it came, it might have so debilitated the contestants as to eliminate Europe and Asia as power factors, thus catapulting the United States into world leadership. But if such a showdown were to result in a clear Russian defeat, the United States and Germany would probably have been left as the polar powers, and world domination might possibly have been within Germany's reach. In other words, a Russian policy that was more palatable to the West might have been riskier than the one actually adopted.

Once the defeat of Germany seemed assured, the Soviet Union's long-range endeavors were chiefly directed toward securing a leading position in the bipolar postwar world. In a sense, this aim reflected the realism of the Russians in estimating their capabilities, which clearly did not justify the expectation that they could forge ahead of the United States in the near future. The Russian estimates were reinforced by the Marxian assumption of an irreconcilable division of the world between the capitalist and socialist camps, which automatically reduced the wartime alliance to a temporary expedient.

Such considerations may explain why the Russians should have given as much attention to political problems as they did, and why these problems often seemed to loom larger, even in the most adverse military situations, than military problems. Even in the midst of the war, Russian policy was clearly oriented toward the postwar world, and the paramount concern with control over Eastern Europe was caused more by long-range political considerations than by immediate tactical ones. It was for this reason that Stalin, with increasing truculence, demanded the postwar incorporation of the Baltic states into the Soviet Union. Evidently, such tangible interests had more real meaning to him than the lofty, but for the time being unattainable, Marxian goal of world domination. He was not, however, so unrealistic as to expect that the Allies would recognize his desired extension of Russian frontiers without receiving something in return; thus, he was prepared to offer a *quid pro quo*. Much to his surprise, his attempts at a businesslike settlement were rebuffed by the American government, which found the substitution of "deals" for principles distasteful. But Stalin was not to be deterred. In the same vein, he confronted his partners at the Yalta meeting with a *fait accompli* in Eastern Europe at a time when Russian forces had reached the Oder River and American prestige had suffered a severe blow because of the Ardennes offensive.

If there was anything unrealistic in the Russian policy, it was misjudgment of the American mentality. Perhaps, it was reasonable to assume that Americans, like other men, were aiming at world domination, or would at least endeavor to reduce the Soviet Union's power position. But when the facts failed to bear out this assumption, Russian leaders did nothing to adjust the presuppositions on which their policy was based. The unhappy result was that instead of bipolar harmony the cold war ensued.

The United States' Responsibility

Perhaps the chief contribution to the shaping of the new order was made by the United States. Although the American role in the war stands out clearly, its underlying motivations and alternatives are not as easy to assess. The effect of the geographic separation of the American continent from both Europe and Asia upon American political thought and policies is well known. But other influences can also be cited to explain some of the peculiarities of American foreign policy. In particular, the power of public opinion, to which political institutions force American leaders to defer, has frequently introduced an element of unrealism into foreign policy. Above all, it gave rise to the illusion that the United States could indefinitely remain aloof from European affairs if it conducted itself with the needed circumspection.

These debilities of American foreign policy did not, to be sure, have any bearing upon Germany's fateful decision to attack the Soviet Union, which was largely responsible for setting off the rapid development of American and Soviet power. The United States was in no position to exercise a restraining influence upon Germany even if it had wanted to do so. However, there were other areas in which more propitious policies were possible and which could have minimized some of the difficulties that were to arise after the war. The preoccupation with securing peace in the postwar world through a frontal assault upon the balance of power and the erection of an international security organization had rendered American leaders insensitive to postwar territorial arrangements and to the problem of the distribution of power. To be sure, American leaders were not alone in this neglect. Churchill foresaw, in the later part of the war, the political difficulties that would follow the cessation of hostilities and tried to soften the effect as much as possible. But in the early stages of the war, when the British were desperately fighting on many widely scattered fronts, he had not given much thought to these problems. When the British finally addressed themselves to the practical problems of peacemaking, their prognosis of the world of the future was far more astute than that of American statesmen.

The most fateful decision made by American leaders during the war was not to negotiate a peace but to force the enemy into unconditional surrender. The elimination by the war of Germany as an effective power could only draw a victorious Soviet Union deep into the heart of Europe. Nevertheless the situation might have been avoided had the unconditional surrender formula been accompanied by a thrust of the Western forces into Berlin—a move American political and military leaders had little sympathy for. Not even Churchill's untiring efforts could convince them that now that the war had been won the postwar distribution of power was the most important issue. Actually, there were neither military nor legal reasons to prevent a drive to the German capital. Apparently, the chief obstacle was the importance attached by American military leaders to vague and rather absurd rumors spread by the Nazis that they were building a National Redoubt in the Alps, from which they would carry on guerrilla operations after their country's defeat. In view of such alarming news, Berlin appeared a target of secondary importance, and the major effort was directed at cutting off the Alpine area. It is also possible that the oft-mentioned jealousy of the American generals vis-à-vis their British comrades was a factor in making the unfortunate decision to turn the Allied armies southward rather than eastward for fear that the British would get the credit for the prestigious capture of the enemy's capital. Whatever the actual reasons, American policy displayed an inability to anticipate the political circumstances of the postwar world.

The political difficulties of the postwar years might have been greatly reduced by a negotiated settlement with the enemy. In this way a power vacuum where Germany had stood would have been avoided. A further precaution against the destruction of the balance of power would have been an Allied invasion of the Balkans. Churchill entertained such a plan, but in spite of its obvious merits it met with Roosevelt's disapproval. To stop Stalin's increasingly transparent expansionist ambitions, the British leader favored operations in southeastern Europe of sufficient scope to maintain the influence of the Western democracies there.[3] In all probability such operations would have pushed the Iron Curtain farther to the east and put the Anglo-American alliance in a stronger strategic and political position in the postwar world. Although the ultimate responsibility for the course followed was Roosevelt's, it must be said in his defense that he acted largely on the recommendation of his military advisors, who were apprehensive of military operations in the difficult Balkan terrain and favored the pursuit of the invasion of France with all the strength the Western alliance could muster. The preference of the generals happily coincided with Roosevelt's own reluctance, in view of the imminent Presidential election, to risk a failure of the attack on France by siphoning off part of the Allied striking force.[4] Although the apprehensions of the military were understandable, the passing up of the political advantages that might have accrued from Churchill's plan had unfortunate consequences: Stalin won the first major battle of the cold war.

A negotiated settlement with the enemy powers, an invasion of the Balkans by the Western Allies, a United Nations guided by regional organizations, and a more judicious pace of American demobilization would not in and by themselves have halted or reversed the trend toward the bipolarization of power. They would have produced greater stability during postwar international relations and placed the United States in a better strategic position. Instead, American statesmen decided to try new methods that they considered more promising. Roosevelt apparently did not attribute the disagreements that had arisen between the Soviet Union and the Western Allies to a fundamental clash of interests. He apparently saw the basis as an unfounded suspicion of Western motives by the Russians, which he thought he could overcome by humoring Stalin. He did not judge it impossible to convert the Russian leader into a useful member of the new world, whose *leitmotif* was cooperation rather than competition. His optimistic appraisal of the future of American-Russian relations made the President receptive to Russian claims concerning postwar territorial settlements. Apparently, he deemed it wise to cement big power amity before incipient tensions created an unbridgeable gap.

The sequel to Roosevelt's efforts to secure Stalin's cooperation in executing his plan for a better world was the agreements reached at Yalta. No doubt these agreements were a source of embarrassment to the United States and, conversely, enhanced the Soviet Union's moral and political stature in the postwar world. However, there is no basis for the charge that Roosevelt made a "deal" at Yalta. Actually, the agreements were not much more than the formal statement of an already existing situation. Little was given away that the Russians did not already have or that could possibly be wrested from them. Moreover, the temporary success of the German Ardennes offensive had put the United States in an unfavorable bargaining position and made Russian friendship appear especially desirable. The only charge that can possibly be made against Roosevelt is that he was laboring under an illusion if he expected that by satisfying their demands he could dissuade the Russians from extending their power beyond the actual frontiers of their country.[5]

THE ALTERNATIVES

There still remains the question whether any alternatives to bipolarity were available. It appears, in retrospect, that the causes of the bipolarization reach back to the days before the war when, for various reasons, the opportunity to take effective precautions was missed. There might not have been a war had the Soviet Union refrained from signing the nonaggression pact with Germany; had the United States refrained from encouraging Hitler through the enactment of neutrality legislation; and had Hitler refrained from gambling so recklessly. With the commencement of the war, the die had been cast, and there is little reason to believe that a more realistic American policy could have prevented the emergence of two polar powers. Although it is idle to deny that the responsibility for permitting Germany to break the power of Great Britain and France in 1940 rests heavily upon the United States, American lack of military preparedness at that time precluded effective intercession. The United States, like other Western democracies, had refused to accept the development of German military power, and relied more on its luck than on its military strength. It has also been argued that the United States erred in helping build up the Soviet Union to the point of making it equal militarily. The Soviet Union should have been given just enough aid to keep it in the war; however, Churchill and Roosevelt, the argument runs, were so blinded by their hatred of Germany that they lost all perspective.[6] There is some merit in these charges, but they ignore the inordinate risk involved in niggardly rationing aid to the Soviet Union. It would, at best, have been a dangerous gamble to put the Eastern ally on an allowance that would barely enable him to keep his armies in the field. The difficulty of determining how much aid was necessary might have placed the Soviet forces in so untenable a position as to leave the Russian government no choice but to sue for a separate peace or, even worse, to surrender unconditionally. This was a chance American leaders knew they could ill afford to take. If Germany succeeded in defeating the Soviet Union and destroying the British Empire, the United States would have been faced with the alternatives of either desperately fighting on alone or bowing to Hitler's "New Order." In either event, there was the risk of being reduced to the level of a second-rate power. The enormity of the Nazi threat made maximum aid to the Soviet Union a practical necessity even if this created a rival strong enough to prevent an antifascist union under American leadership after the war.

The wisdom of pursuing the war until Germany's unconditional surrender is more doubtful. The psychology behind that decision is understandable. It was widely felt that the resurgence of German militarism so soon after defeat in the First World War could in large measure be attributed to the popular myth in Germany that the German army had been undefeated on the field of battle but had been stabbed in the back by the homefront. The revival of that myth in relation to the Second World War was to be effectively blocked by total military collapse. It was also hoped that a firm commitment to the unconditional surrender formula would help assuage fears within the anti-German alliance that separate peace negotiations were underway. All these were good reasons; but they were not enough to neutralize the impracticality of the formula. To be sure, the extinction of a country's sovereignty had not been an unknown practice in the past. What was strange about the decision made at Casablanca—and it seems to have caused considerable consternation among some American leaders including Secretary of State Cordell Hull—was the casualness with which the question of filling the power vacuum that would follow Germany's military and political collapse was treated.[7] The Allied agreement to dismember Germany and to detach East Prussia and the lands east of the Oder River further played into the hands of the Russians, and thus cleared the way for the subsequent bipolarization of power. Since a long-range strategic rationale cannot be found, the decision was probably an immediate political and psychological necessity and appeared reasonable as the sequel to a war in which political considerations were subordinated to ideological ones.

Once Soviet ambitions had become apparent to Western leaders and the wartime harmony had given way to political rivalry, the acrimony of the bipolar struggle was heightened by the difference in the overall objectives of the two sides. While the Western Allies were aiming at restoring and perpetuating an economically, socially, and, to a degree, politically obsolete status quo, the Soviet Union was hoping to change the world by appealing to the smouldering forces that had been unleashed by the war. It held out the promise of wiping out poverty, insecurity, toil, and ignorance. By contrast, aid to established governments appeared to align the United States firmly on the side of the old order. The lines dividing the world into two camps were, thus, sharply drawn.

Can it be said, then, that the United States should have followed a course other than the one it actually chose? It could, of course, be maintained that the United States might have prevented the bipolarization of power by proceeding with more caution and cunning during the war. For example, if the United States could not prevent the advance of Soviet forces into or drive them back from Central Europe, it was unwise to permit German military power to collapse. Less wholehearted support of the Soviet Union and a peace with Germany while the latter's military machine was still intact, though risky, might have preserved a multiple balance. Such a balance would probably have been less highly differentiated than the prewar balance, but at least it would have had the advantage of not being afflicted with the debilities of bipolarism. However, it is doubtful that such a course would have been safe or advisable. While it might have jeopardized victory by undermining Allied unity, it would not have prevented the enormous strides made by the United States and the Soviet Union in armament technology, on which the unique power positions of these two countries rests. Nothing could have prevented the rise of Soviet power to its present position as long as the Soviet Union was among the victorious nations. Had it been defeated by Germany, the latter undoubtedly would have emerged as one of the two leading powers in the bipolar world. There is, therefore, no basis for reproaching the United States for aligning itself as it did. However, if that alignment was to lead inevitably to bipolarism, the United States might have been more far-sighted than it was in securing its position in the postwar world. It is here that American statesmanship was wanting.

CHAPTER THREE

COLD WAR AND COEXISTENCE

The history of the cold war has been well covered, and numerous observers have provided us with perceptive analyses. However, such analyses have generally suffered from a tendency to tell the story in personal terms —of good men fighting bad men—giving scant attention to the tragic predicament that has often rendered cold war problems insolvable. These interpretations would remove the cold war problem through mutual concessions and agreement. Unfortunately, there is little basis to support the assumption that consensus of reasonable and well-intentioned men is all that is needed to remove the prevailing tensions. The assumption neglects the long-range forces involved in shaping the course of historical events that are too obdurate to be reversed by simple fiat. The inclination to magnify the role of free individual decision is not without practical danger. Disappointed hopes for a lasting peace can easily lead otherwise reasonable men into recklessness. Such frustrations, if ascribed to the malevolence or unreasonableness of the opponent, may alternately produce a crusading spirit and a defeatist mood. An examination of the impersonal forces inherent in the political setting is necessary to eliminate such dangers.

THE NATURE OF THE COLD WAR

The drastic change that has occurred in international relations precludes an analysis of the cold war in terms of the familiar categories of peace and war. The state of affairs normally referred to as "cold war" is neither war in the technical legal sense nor is it peace in actuality. The fierce opposition of the two hostile blocs is a condition that seems to merit special categorization as a peculiarity of the bipolar system. The unprecedented extent of military preparations, the restricted possibilities of maneuver, and the clearly drawn fronts require new analytical categories. The enormous advance in armament technology further emphasizes the uniqueness of the present condition and impresses its peculiar stamp upon it. The new technology has also added a curious contradiction in that it has involved the superpowers in a compulsive competition for the most modern implements of war, although neither expects to make actual use of them. The prodigious potential for destruction of contemporary arms provides a strong incentive to the hostile parties to avoid a military clash and to accommodate themselves to some form of coexistence. This is not to say that a military clash cannot or will not occur. But the cold war contest is, in essence, political and limited military clashes, if they do occur, are of secondary importance. Full-fledged nuclear war lies beyond the realm of political calculation, and the power struggle takes place in the political arena rather than on the battlefield.

The skeptic may question whether the concept of "cold war" is sufficiently real to warrant such special consideration. Does the term actually signify anything different from the tense state of nonbelligerency normally called peace? Does it, perhaps, reflect the prevalent utopian view that looks upon peace as a condition of general blessedness in which good-neighborliness has extinguished all mistrust of one's fellowmen? On closer inspection, real differences between peace and cold war emerge. The major difference is the subjective feeling of the powers that they are not at peace and that peace is neither attainable nor perhaps even desirable. Even though fear of new and untested weapons has generated an unprecedented reluctance to go to war, the contest has, nonetheless, all the seriousness and intensity of open warfare. As in all major wars, the atmosphere is pervaded by a certainty that there is no alternative to the relentless struggle, whatever the consequences may be. Acrimony is further heightened by the intense ideological competition that is part of the political contest between the two power blocs.

Goals, intensity, and attitudes put the cold war solidly in the category of war. It seems, therefore, misleading to view it as a "twilight zone between peace and war," as President Eisenhower chose to call it.[1] The absence of military action by itself is no crucial test. The employment of military means has never been an indispensable or reliable criterion of war. The Second World War, for example, did not see any military clash between Germany and the Western Allies during the first eight months, and yet it could not seriously be denied that these countries were at war. Conversely, the United States has undertaken numerous military forays into Central America without being at war. It would seem, therefore, that war can take many forms and that there may be real and effective warfare that does not meet the legal requirements of war. If the uneasy situation created by persistent and frequently aggravated tensions between the competing blocs is neither peace in fact nor war in the technical legal or military sense, it is nonetheless a real political war. Because of the substitution of the ideological contest for the military one and of guerrilla fighters for organized armies, it has, in fact, come to resemble what may be called international civil war. Warfare of this type, permeating as it does all phases of life and fought in all earnestness for the highest stakes, can hardly be considered an intermediate stage. The fact that the contestants are motivated less by appetites for territorial conquest than by an irrepressible fear of the adversary's power and ambition in no way diminishes the seriousness of their purpose and permits only gloomy prospects for any genuine reconciliation.

THE COLD WAR PATTERN

Phases of the Cold War

The cold war began with the cessation of hostilities in 1945. Since then it has passed through a number of phases which may conveniently be distinguished. The first phase was marked by unilateral Soviet provocations, which belatedly alerted the United States to the changes that had occurred. Initially, American leaders attributed the quickly rising tensions between the erstwhile Allies to a mutual misunderstanding of each other's view of the world rather than to the redistribution of power. Although Stalin had been farsighted enough to anticipate political peculiarities of the postwar world, his analysis was defective in other respects; he failed to understand that Americans were entirely serious about their attack on the balance of power and were unwilling to accept the new distribution of power as irreversible. It is understandable that Stalin should have found American thinking more than a little enigmatic. Even a less conspiratorial mind would have responded with distrust to the American refusal to agree to mutual accommodation of power interests, which, under the circumstances, appeared legitimate to Stalin. Although it is unlikely that such accommodation, had it been agreed upon, would have cleared the road to perpetual friendship, the American slowness to comprehend the new political situation and the Russian inability to understand the American mentality unduly sharpened the acrimony of the bipolar contest.

The first clouds in Russo-American relations appeared soon after Yalta when the Soviet Union reneged on its commitments concerning the political reconstruction of Poland. Further incidents increased American suspicions. The Soviet Union refused to withdraw its forces from Persia; Communist Albania planted mines in the Corfu Channel causing the destruction of a British warship; the Soviet Union pressed its territorial demands against Turkey, and claimed a share of the former Italian colonies in

North Africa. American statesmen were alarmed by such apparently unfriendly acts. The developing tensions were all the more disconcerting in view of the enormous prestige the Soviet Union had gained in Europe through its impressive military accomplishments during the war. In light of these events, it was not surprising that American reaction was one of incipient enmity and distrust.

There is little reason to be surprised at Soviet stirrings after Germany's defeat. Unlike the United States, which had emerged from the war as the strongest power, the Soviet Union was far from content with its position. Even the elimination of the German threat had given it less security than it had wished for, and the future still seemed to hold much uncertainty. The former hostility of the Western powers was vividly remembered, and the friendliness of the immediate neighbors could not be taken for granted. A considerable amount of handiwork, therefore, was required to bring about a more favorable distribution of power. The problem seemed to reach alarming proportions after Secretary of State James Byrnes' conciliatory Stuttgart Address in September 1946, which appeared as a first step toward grooming former enemies for partnership in an alliance that could only be anti-Soviet in aim. Soviet activism was further enhanced by dynamic ideology, military success, the existence of a power vacuum in adjacent areas that it would be risky to leave unfilled, and the age-old Russian need for warm water ports.

Although Soviet motives are easy to understand, the United States could hardly be expected to remain passive for long in face of the Russian disturbances. Thus, the first phase quickly gave way to the second phase—bilateral aggressiveness. American statesmen at last became aware that they had been passive for too long and had been too willing, in the interest of prolonging the Allied honeymoon, to make concessions that were hard to justify in terms of American interests. While these thoughts were jelling in the minds of American leaders, the Soviet Union missed no opportunity to undermine the position of its former allies. The formula that the United States adopted to counteract Soviet maneuvers was simple: The status quo was to be defended against all Russian and communist attempts to upset it. The American position would be weakened, it was felt, by a change in the existing order of things. Thus, the Grand Alliance split into two camps assuming the roles of defender and challenger of the status quo.

By 1947, disagreements had deteriorated into open enmity. To deter further Soviet inroads in noncommunist parts of the world, the United States openly proclaimed a policy of containing not only Soviet territorial expansion but also the spread of communist regimes. The first action taken was the extension of military and economic aid to Greece and Turkey to help them defend their territorial integrity and stabilize their governments. Soon after, economic aid was extended to Western and Central Europe to arrest the political gains of indigenous communist forces. At the same time, the Russians set out to consolidate their control over Eastern Europe by establishing local communist governments. They also tried to nullify wartime agreements concerning the presence of Western occupation forces in Berlin in an attempt to consolidate their sphere of influence. But they did not stop here; they undertook to break out of the confinement of American containment by encouraging disturbances outside their orbit. As a result, war ensued in divided Korea after Communist North Korea attacked South Korea. When the war ended in a stalemate, the theater of action shifted to Indochina where the natives, with communist support, rose against French colonial rule. In 1951, Tibet came under the domination of Communist China. And additional communist disturbances occurred in other parts of Southeast Asia.

This course of events differed appreciably from Allied expectations before the end of the Second World War. But United States' disillusionment over Stalin's unreliability as a partner in building a better world was probably no greater than Stalin's disappointment at the American refusal to play the part of an honest crook. Stalin seemed quite willing, for example, to respect the interests of the Western Allies in Greece; but when the United States and Great Britain raised questions concerning political developments in Rumania and Poland, he bitterly resented what he considered to be interference in his sphere of influence. The inevitable result was the closing of the anti-Soviet bloc. Although the United States was enjoying a temporary monopoly in atomic weapons, its military advantage was hardly sufficient for it to reshape the world in its own image. It, therefore, responded politically by building alliances in various geographic areas. The tangible value of surrounding the Soviet Union with a network of alliances may be open to argument, and certainly varied from case to case. But to ordered minds, it corresponded ideally to the officially proclaimed policy of containment.

Western alliances were consolidated and extended at the same time that economic and political reconstruction was fostered by the Marshall Plan and a scheme for European integration. The Soviet Union was equally busy consolidating Eastern Europe by redrawing frontiers with its neighbors and by establishing communist governments wherever possible. At the same time, the United States attempted to strengthen the resistance of uncommitted countries to Soviet influence. Although this had to be done largely through ideological and economic means, the American policy of containment set off unprecedented peacetime activity in both military and foreign policies. In accepting the communist challenge of world domination, the United States permitted defense expenditures and establishments to assume enormous proportions, despite the fact that the Soviet Union had not conquered any territory from 1948 to 1958.

By the early 1950's, the American feeling of strategic superiority had been profoundly shaken by the explosion of a Russian atomic bomb, followed later by the successful launching of a Russian satellite. Further ground for concern was the instability of the political balance, thrown into confusion during the 1950's by a series of nationalist revolutions in underdeveloped areas. Under these conditions, mutual accommodation was sought. There was reason to hope that a de facto compromise might be reached between the Big Two, ensuring a hands-off policy in each other's sphere of influence. Encouraging signs were not lacking. Chiang

Kai-shek, who had been "put on a leash" by President Truman in 1950 to curb his designs on the Chinese mainland, and who had been "unleashed" by President Eisenhower in 1953 in response to domestic political pressures in the United States, was "releashed" in 1954, lest he create embarrassments for American foreign policy. In 1955, Eastern and Western Allies signed a peace treaty with Austria, containing provisions for Austrian neutrality. And a general feeling of optimism prevailed, due to the beneficent effects of foreign ministers meetings and summit conferences. However, all hopes ended with the Suez crisis and the Hungarian uprising. It was not to be expected that the Russians would leave the Middle East crisis unexploited, since participation in the settlement of the dispute promised rich rewards, either by gaining the gratitude and affection of the Arab countries or by rocking the Western alliance. They may hardly have anticipated that both goals would be achieved with one stroke. The United States, on the other hand, could not afford to remain disinterested in the Hungarian episode. Although there were definite limits to the possibility of concrete American action, the United States went on record sharply condemning Soviet ruthlessness.

The end of the era of good feeling and hopefulness was officially signaled in 1957 by the Eisenhower Doctrine, which expressed the willingness of the United States to give military assistance, if requested, to any Middle East victim of communist aggression. The chief importance of the doctrine lay in the implied admission that accommodation was not a practical possibility in relations between the Big Two. One may, in fact, doubt that the Russians seriously entertained hopes of accommodation after the Americans refused to play according to the rules. It is quite likely that, in seeming to enter into the hopeful spirit that was radiating through the Western world, they were merely trying to exploit the advantages American self-delusion was providing.

Once the Suez situation was under control, competition again became the keynote of international politics and, as the cold war spread, was felt in all spheres of activity, from the military to the economic to the scientific realm.

Competition also spread geographically. Although the
prime targets have been the uncommitted areas in Asia
and Africa, the Soviet Union attempted to establish foot
holds in the opponent's camp by carrying the competition
into the Western hemisphere. In general, both sides have
been trying to reach their goals in the struggle for people's
minds and, consequently, have directed extraordinary ef
forts to the field of propaganda.

Trouble Spots

The intense competition of the Big Two has produced
trouble spots that have not only been irritants but have
been possible causes of global conflagration; Yugoslavia
and Cuba are both good examples of such tinderboxes
Yugoslavia became a source of irritation in 1949 when the
United States decided to extend aid in order to encourage
the country's disaffection from the Soviet Union. The
United States has been similarly provoked by the rap
prochement between Cuba and the Soviet Union since the
Castro revolution. Although in contrast to Cuba Yugo
slavia did not shift to the opposing side, there is some
similarity in the reactions of the two leading powers. Fol
lowing the pattern of American policy in the Yugosla
episode, the Soviet Union has promised military suppor
to the Caribbean island against possible American attempt
to encroach upon its territorial integrity. Although both
instances were potentially explosive, the problems were
resolved peaceably since neither side felt overly justified in
insisting on its presence in the adversary's camp.

Far more persistent and dangerous are certain clearl
anomalous, though less unambiguous, situations that, a
some time, will require a solution. Such irritants have
arisen either from arrangements made before the bipola
balance had become fully articulated or, after new situa
tions had arisen, from the inability of the superpowers t
reach agreement regarding certain disputed areas. For ex
ample, Quemoy and Matsu, and Formosa and Berlin ar
strong outposts of the anticommunist alliance and there
fore are, and are likely to remain, sore spots in a divide

world. Yet there is little likelihood that the most peace-loving men will be able to agree upon a settlement even in strategically insignificant areas since the rigidity of bipolar politics leaves little room for territorial change or adjustment. This is a melancholy circumstance in many ways for which it is easier to find an explanation than a solution. The dilemma arises from the unwillingness of either side to yield on any matter of substance because every loss to one side is a dual gain to the other, which profits not only to the extent of its gain but also to the extent of the opponent's loss. Attempts have, nevertheless, been made to find solutions of some kind. One example is the neutralization of Laos, which, it was hoped, would resolve the stalemate in Indochina. Unfortunately, such hopes came to naught. Directly in the path of the communist advance in Southeast Asia, Laos has remained a target of communist pressures, emanating either from Moscow or Peking. Although the country has no direct strategic significance, the United States could not remain indifferent to its fate. The effect that Laotian surrender would have on the American political position in Southeast Asia, and perhaps elsewhere, leave the United States little choice but to insist on Laos' continued neutrality and to support the forces that are willing to resist communist subversive activity.

The attempted solution of the Indochina crisis has broken down completely in Vietnam. The ensuing armed conflict involves not only the contending Vietnamese factions but also the United States. The American action cannot be explained in terms of nonobservance of agreements by the North Vietnamese or legal or moral commitments to South Vietnam, since the United States was not a party to the Geneva agreement of 1954 concerning the reunification of Vietnam. Moreover, of the two Vietnamese factions, the responsibility for the war probably lies more heavily with the South. However, considerations of cold war strategy provide a number of weighty reasons for American participation. The United States is fearful that a communist takeover of South Vietnam would encourage communist "wars of liberation" elsewhere and would merely be a prelude to the abandonment of Southeast Asia to implacably hostile forces. Furthermore, American leaders are apprehensive of the effect that surrender of Vietnam would have both on the communist and noncommunist world. Within the communist world, any apparent display of weakness by the United States would inevitably encourage the belligerent factions. In the noncommunist world, the allies, especially in Asia, would be demoralized, while the uncommitted would cease to take American power seriously. Moreover, the impression of unreliability or impotence would drive countries that are now relying on promises of American protection to develop nuclear striking forces of their own. However desirable it may be for the United States to extricate itself from the Vietnam imbroglio, it does not appear practical to surrender important strategic assets.

The difficulties arising in the Congo after independence was granted by Belgium in June 1960 were of more than local interest. The combination of anti-Westernism and separatism threatened to create the kind of chaos that would open the gates to Soviet influence. The United States, therefore, had an obvious interest in securing the orderly transition from colony to independent state, and to prevent the Balkanization of the continent. These have also been the goals of the United Nations action undertaken at the request of the Congolese government. Since the interposition of international forces adversely affected the Soviet interest in generating confusion, it was regarded by the Russians and native groups alike as a prop of Western anticommunist and colonial strategy.

By far the thorniest problem facing the Big Two is the status of Berlin. Inasmuch as this Western enclave within the Soviet sphere is the only remaining anomaly in divided Europe, it has easily been the most explosive issue in the bipolar world. The city's status is clearly incompatible with the bipolar tendency toward rigid divisions. The dispute is especially heated because it is in Germany that the interests of the antagonists clash most vitally, and the dividing line, except for Berlin, is drawn most sharply. The continued focus of cold war issues on Europe may, perhaps, occasion surprise in view of the superpowers' absorbing concern with extra-European areas, which today are the most prominent arenas of cold war battles. Such a shift of the cold war theater does not, however, mean the end of Europe's importance in the contest. The improbability of a decision on Berlin and the self-assertion of European states against big power tutelage have caused the antagonists to tread cautiously and to avoid dramatic upsets. Europe, nevertheless, continues to be a cause of anxiety and the object of unrelenting attention because of its geographic proximity and because here the Iron Curtain has been rung down clearly and irrevocably. The faintest suggestion of any change along such a clearly-drawn dividing line is therefore likely to create a major upset of the bipolar order and to have global repercussions.

The Berlin question may also shed some light on the possibility of a general settlement of cold war issues. The specific grievances were stated in a Soviet note of November 27, 1958. The Soviet Union, in essence, justified its demands for a change in the city's status as follows: the position of Berlin as a state within a state was said to be a legal and political absurdity; equally absurd was the apparent intent of the Western powers to perpetuate the military occupation of the city; the Soviet Union felt harrassed by Western intelligence and espionage activities as well as acts of sabotage, based in West Berlin, against the East German Republic and Soviet forces stationed there; and finally it was suggested that the isolation of Berlin had resulted in West Berlin's failure to realize its economic potential.[2] The concrete demands of the Soviet Union have not, however, gone so far as to insist on the outright incorporation of West Berlin into the East German People's Republic. Rather, the attainment of Soviet goals has been attempted through more subtle proposals, such as the immediate conclusion of a peace treaty with Germany, the establishment of West Berlin as a demilitarized free city, and the termination of the rights of the Western Allies in the city. In rejecting these proposals the United States has rested its case on its legal right, established by treaty, to maintain forces in Berlin and on its moral obligation to ensure the city's freedom. It has therefore aimed at maintaining the status quo if possible, but as a minimum has insisted on its free access and the city's continued independence.

The legal merits of the issue are far from clear. Neither is the American position entirely sound, as George Kennan has pointed out,[3] nor are Soviet objections to the continuation of the status quo as outrageously cynical as they may appear at first sight. It is doubtful that the 1945 agreements, on which the Western claims are based, are still binding in view of violations by both sides.[4] Moreover, one cannot dismiss the Soviet contention that the treaty has been invalidated by the great changes that have occurred in world politics since its inception and that a military occupation in perpetuity is a patent absurdity. In situations of this kind, general international law does, in fact, permit unilateral abrogation of treaty obligations. Although the permissiveness of this rule may cause serious misgivings because of its destructive effect upon the binding force of international law, it is nonetheless a valid rule. Even if the legal issues were to be untangled through adjudication, it is highly improbable that this would resolve the political issues that are the basis of the controversy. It is interesting to observe that neither side has seriously proposed adjudication. Apparently, both know only too well that compliance with an adverse court decision would not be politically feasible and that the legal issues involved are too debatable to permit a reasonable prediction of the outcome. In the meantime, one of the two key legal issues—the status of the city as a whole—has been resolved unilaterally by the Soviet Union through the erection of the Berlin Wall. The other issue, Western access to Berlin, remains.

The political interests of the Soviet Union in liquidating Berlin's postwar status are varied. They arise partly from the need to strengthen the Soviet political position within its own camp and partly from a desire to undermine the anticommunist alliance forged by the United States. The Soviet Union has been greatly embarrassed vis-à-vis its own satellites by the continued presence of Western forces on its side of the Iron Curtain, which may easily be interpreted as an indication of Soviet weakness. Moreover, Soviet prestige has suffered as a result of the splendid example of West Germany's economic recovery, which is on open display in West Berlin. A further source of embarrassment has been the numerous escapes of East German citizens to the West, made possible by the international administration of Berlin. A display of power by the Soviet Union to counteract the heavy loss of prestige may be a practical necessity. The erection of the Berlin Wall was, to some extent, that show of strength. But Soviet prestige would, no doubt, be further enhanced if the Allies could be forced to recognize the East German satellite *de jure*. Forcing the Allies out of Berlin would have the further advantages of strengthening Communist Party leadership at home and abroad, of alleviating Eastern European fears of West Germany, and of shaking off the deleterious economic effects of the Western presence in Berlin, which the Soviet Union complained of in its note of August 18, 1961 rejecting the Western protest against the closing of the border between East and West Berlin.[5]

These motives are understandable enough. But if political circumstances force the Soviet Union to press for a change in Berlin's status, they leave the United States no choice but to resist. To defer to Russian demands would have a profoundly harmful effect upon the stability of the American bloc. It would destroy European confidence in the United States, thus eliminating American influence on European affairs. But what actually gives the Berlin affair its importance in contemporary international politics is the fact that, aside from the substantive issues involved, it is a test of the determination of the United States to defend its position in Europe, with force if necessary. Consequently, any action that could possibly be interpreted as a sign of weakness would not only result in more far-reaching demands, but would immeasurably enhance the possibility of nuclear war by, eventually, reducing American alternatives to surrender to Soviet blackmail or war.

The apparent irresponsibility of the Soviet Union, in periodically stirring up the Berlin issue, and of the United States, in refusing even to consider any proposal of a change, can be rationally explained. It is Berlin's political rather than strategic importance that has precluded a settlement and accounts for the explosive potentialities of the issue. It is difficult to see any way out of the impasse, which could lead to universal tragedy, even if both sides were reasonably well intentioned. To be sure, President Kennedy declared on July 23, 1961, that the United States was not "wedded to any particular arrangement," and indicated his willingness to discuss changes in the city's status as well as an all-German peace treaty. But he left no doubt that the United States would not tolerate unilateral Soviet action or complete communist control over Berlin, which the Soviet Union covets. It is conceivable that the problem might be solved by a new arrangement that would accommodate Soviet interests in return for concessions of equal value to the United States in other areas. However, to avoid upsetting the existing political balance, the United States would have to drive a hard bargain. In view of the moral zeal of bipolar diplomacy, it is unlikely that the Soviet Union would be prepared to make adequate concessions to satisfy American interests. Ideological and moral commitments have restrained the freedom of action of both contestants so as to preclude concessions of any consequence. Moreover, the United States has won some minor victories in recent years. The President's arguments in terms of national self-determination have evoked favorable reactions among the Africans and Asians, and the mass migrations of East Germans to the West have greatly improved the image of the United States everywhere. There is little wonder, then, that the United States should be unwilling to give up such advantages. The fact that such gains have largely been lost due to the American conduct of the war in Vietnam has hardly rendered the United States more willing to surrender positions. The Soviet Union, in turn, may feel that it can retrieve some of its propaganda losses by alternately precipitating crises over Berlin and launching peace offensives. In this way, a pious image of Soviet power, one that considers no price too high to save the peace, can be presented to the world. Even if the Soviet

Union entertains no serious hopes that the Berlin issue may be solved to its satisfaction, the game is not without danger. The tenuous line between cold and hot war may not be able to stand the continuous strain, and eventually tensions may become sufficiently unbearable to bring forth military attempts to solve the impasse.

Fluctuations in the Balance of Power

For all its rigidity, the bipolar balance of power is delicate and, paradoxically, subject to considerable fluctuation in areas that are geographically and politically removed from the polar powers. The need to maintain an approximate equilibrium between the destructive capabilities of the two blocs has made the superpowers exceedingly sensitive to change and susceptible to considerable nervousness and perhaps even recklessness. Moreover, their eagerness to improve their political position by luring newcomers into their respective blocs has introduced an element of instability into generally rigid power alignments. Considerable fluctuation was observed immediately after the Second World War when the two blocs were consolidating and Eastern Europe and China joined the Soviet camp. Since then, fundamental changes have occurred in former colonial areas, such as Indochina and a number of uncommitted countries, particularly in the Middle East. Other nations, like sub-Saharan Africa and India, are vacillating while still trying to maintain independent positions. The competition for allies has been and remains lively. To be sure, the failure of the United States to establish amicable relations with China in an effort to prevent its close alignment with the Soviet Union constituted a departure from the general rule. An attempt to drive a wedge between the communist powers, even if it did not succeed, might have been worth a try. Evidently, the United States, unaware of the new political necessities, assigned a higher priority to ideological interests than to political interests. It is doubtful that such misjudgments would occur at a time when the bipolar balance has become so clearly articulated.

CAN THE COLD WAR BE LIQUIDATED?

Mankind's longing for the termination of the cold war has become increasingly emphatic. A settlement is a matter of greatest urgency, but it has been curiously obstructed by the very fear from which the urgency derives, and which has dimmed the chances for an overall settlement short of a general war. Any attempts to relax international tension are immediately confronted by formidable difficulties arising from the contradictory aims pursued by the superpowers. American policy has been directed toward maintaining the status quo while the Soviet Union has set out to revise it. These divergent aims have developed historically as a concomitant of bipolarization. It was natural that as the bipolar balance emerged, one of the two leading powers was the stronger, which was true of the United States at the end of the Second World War. It is equally natural for the stronger power to want to maintain its advantageous position by preserving the status quo. But it is no less understandable that the lesser of the two powers should exploit all avenues and all weaknesses of the stronger in order to bring about a change.

The United States has attempted to attain its ends through a policy of containing its expansionist and revisionist opponent territorially and ideologically. Although the logic of this policy is impeccable, it is not likely to produce the desired results. Inasmuch as the momentary status quo is rarely equally satisfactory to both sides, the formula cannot be relied upon to promote stability. To improve its security, the Soviet Union has pressed for changes on various fronts in defiance of the American policy, and can be expected to do so in the future. Since the United States, for equally valid security reasons, cannot remain indifferent to such challenges, containment has explosive possibilities.

Aside from such hazards, the rationale of containment is subject to question. It is apparent that such a policy undermines the military position of the containing power by leaving the choice of targets and weapons to the opponent. The more serious defects, however, are the military and territorial aspects of the doctrine. They have little relevance to the cold war that is being fought for the control of men's minds rather than for the acquisition of territorial possessions. As a result, the real problem of ideological and political containment is being bypassed, especially in the underdeveloped areas, where communism is usually an internal rather than an external threat. Not only does it seem unlikely in such circumstances that the line can be held through political and economic actions that are only taken in response to communist activity, but there is also some question as to whom the policy actually contains. By preaching anticommunism, the United States has denied itself the opportunity of extending its influence into countries where political and economic circumstances require communistic solutions rather than democratic-capitalistic methods. In many areas, therefore, the policy has resulted in a self-containment of the United States instead of in the containment of communist powers or movements. Actually, containment has not been of any great practical value in preventing the rise of communist governments in countries outside the acknowledged Soviet orbit. Apparently, a more pliable policy is needed to maintain the status quo.

The possibility that under present political conditions even minor provocations may have catastrophic results has not produced fatalistic resignation. Methods for relaxing tensions have been persistently explored despite discouraging prospects. The stabilization of the bipolar balance by defining the superpowers' respective spheres of influence and control has been considered a theoretical possibility. Although it is far from clear just what Americans expected from summit conferences, the general elation reflected in such slogans as the "spirit of Geneva" and the "spirit of Camp David" seemed to indicate that they entertained hopes for a general settlement. Unfortunately, such hopes rested more on wishful thinking than on hard facts. Neither the United States, committed as it is to the status quo in the international distribution of power, nor the Soviet Union, with its formal commitment to a universalist ideology of terrestrial salvation, is likely to make concessions of the kind that would satisfy the other. Moreover, if an agreement were ever reached, there is little reason to expect that the two powers would indefinitely confine themselves to their respective spheres. Paradoxically, concern with the international status quo has not prevented the United States from advocating, when advantageous, the revolutionary doctrine of national self-determination as a basis for domestic political organization. The adverse effect that national self-determination could have upon the status quo has been obscured by the confident expectation that the magic of democracy would cause nations to choose political forms favorable to the United States. In practice, that expectation has often materialized. The United States would, therefore, find it awkward to cast away so formidable a cold war weapon by entering into agreements along the lines indicated. The result would be to facilitate Soviet intervention in the Eastern bloc and to drive panic-stricken uncommitted countries into the Soviet camp. The sense of despair among the Soviet Union's satellites, the disillusionment of the United States' allies, and the diminishing resistance of third powers to communist pressures, which would be likely to follow from such arrangements, could hardly remain a matter of indifference to the United States.

These difficulties alone may not necessarily rule out all chances of a settlement of some kind. It may appear practical to think in terms of a more modest approach. If international tensions cannot be removed, they can perhaps be alleviated through a mutual recognition of the existing de facto spheres of influence. Unfortunately, such an arrangement would not be likely to dispose of the crucial problem, which is not in Europe, where the dividing line is rather clearly drawn, but in the uncommitted countries of Asia and Africa. Moreover, any agreement to stake out spheres would either have to include a mutual guarantee to respect their integrity or explicit toleration of free competition in these areas; the latter, however, would perpetuate conflict and would, therefore, preclude the stabilization of the bipolar balance. The former would hardly be acceptable to the Soviet Union because of the advantages that communism enjoys in underdeveloped areas.

It has occasionally been suggested that, analogous to the solution of the religious wars, the cold war might be resolved in terms of a variant of the formula *cuius regio eius religio*. Such a solution was feasible, to be sure, when religion was the object of the power struggle. But it has little promise when the object of the power struggle is power, pure and simple. The fear generated when self-sustained power seeks to supplant self-sustained power of equal strength prevents any real concession if there are no third powers capable of effectively interceding. Under such conditions a formula that is indifferent to the distribution of power is not apt to inspire much confidence. Considerations of security do not permit either side to leave the opponent's weaknesses unexploited, or to limit its own military preparations. Consequently, the most attractive proposals are a priori suspect of being Trojan Horses.

Another, much-debated approach is disengagement. One may wonder whether the disentanglement of political involvements is more feasible than containment or staking out of spheres of influence. Mutual guarantees to respect the integrity of uncommitted countries are as much a prerequisite for the working of this scheme as they are for the definition of spheres of influence. In fact, disengagement would add the further and more formidable difficulty of neutralizing Europe. The minimum requirement would be the withdrawal of American forces from Western and Central Europe and Soviet forces from Eastern Europe. Neutralization would also imply the dissolution of NATO and the Warsaw Pact. So large an order, of course, could not be filled with one stroke. But even a modest initial arrangement, if it were to be at all meaningful, could not evade the unification and neutralization of Germany. The execution of such a plan would require more than agreement in principle, and, when the practical problems involved are faced, the obstacles seem virtually insurmountable. One writer has perceptively remarked that disengagement would require the creation of a united Germany that is both democratic and neutral. But "the Russians do not trust a democratic Germany to remain neutral and the West does not trust a neutral Germany to remain democratic." [6]

If a settlement within the bipolar framework is not possible, would it be improvident or absurd to break out of the bipolar strait-jacket? It has often been suggested that the traditional multiple balance be restored in the hope that the many present difficulties can then be resolved by a balancer. However, under present technological conditions, it is doubtful that such a return to previous conditions is possible or advisable. To restore the multiple balance system, it would be necessary to diffuse the nuclear means of mass destruction and the long-range missiles required to deliver the destructive weapons. The possession of such weapons by a growing circle of nations could only multiply the opportunities for mischief, and the chances of a nuclear war would be immeasurably enhanced.

COEXISTENCE

If cold war issues cannot be settled or the balance of power stabilized, the question arises whether the war can be kept cold. Is the cold war a real alternative to both surrender and preventive war, or must it eventually degenerate into a military clash? Can the present balance be expected to last until gradual political developments or technological changes produce a new political system? The danger that the present equilibrium may be upset is real enough. But the impasse reached in the cold war and the improbability that outstanding issues can be resolved militarily has caused both sides to look favorably upon coexistence, not only as a desirable condition for the moment but as a reasonable prospect for an indefinite future.

The Bases of Coexistence

To a large extent, the mutual acceptance of coexistence rests on the deterring effect of the present state of nuclear weapons. The fear that everything may be lost in a nuclear war has thus far prevented existing tensions from erupting. To be sure, the buildup of armaments as deterrents is part of military history. The uniqueness of the present situation is the enormous destructive power of modern armaments, which has created the expectation that neither side can win a war fought with the most up-to-date weapons. This belief is based partly on the nature of nuclear warfare and partly on certain necessary assumptions. Possession of the most formidable means of destruction has not made the nuclear powers immune to attack. No amount of preparation can provide protection for their highly vulnerable cities, and there is reason to suspect that even the countryside would be subject to devastation by a nuclear attack. At the same time, it is unreasonable to expect that such losses can be counterbalanced by crippling the opponent's ability to retaliate effectively. The development of mobile launching sites and automatic mechanisms for setting the full retaliatory force in motion in the event of a massive attack makes a counterblow possible even if an attack upon urban centers were to disrupt the administrative apparatus of the government, the communications system, and the economic order. Opinions as to whether there is an appreciable advantage in a nuclear surprise attack seem to vary. However, the would-be aggressor would have to take into account the likelihood that he could not destroy the opponent's retaliatory force and that in the event of nuclear retribution, he would stand to lose as much as his victim. Under such conditions, victory loses its attraction, and war ceases to be a useful instrument of national policy.

War, then, has declined as an effective tool of foreign policy. The expectation of a military victory can no longer be reasonably entertained by either side. Yet arguments, however rational, give no assurance that the danger of war has been effectively extinguished. Deterrence is not inherent in nuclear weapons but depends on certain conditions. The possibility of an accident occurring can never be wholly eliminated; and there always remains the chance that a limited war may escalate into an all-out nuclear war. Aside from such chance factors, the assumption of enduring coexistence is premised on the exclusive possession of the means of nuclear mass destruction by the United States and the Soviet Union. If there were to be a liberal diffusion of such weapons, it is possible that a gravely discontented member of the nuclear club would prefer a nuclear holocaust to an unbearable status quo.

If the diffusion of nuclear weapons is prevented, there is still no reason to take deterrence for granted. It will be effective only as long as the invulnerability of retaliatory forces is assumed. If, however, there is reason to believe that the opponent's force can be effectively crippled, the temptation to launch a surprise attack will, in the long run, become irresistible. This possibility cannot be dismissed. A technological breakthrough may give one side a decided superiority. Moreover, it is conceivable that political and military situations might arise when an attack may seem to be the only rational course. To minimize such risks it is necessary for the antagonists to maintain scientific research, armament technology, and military establishments at a competitive level. In this way alone can there be a reasonable assurance that any possible advance on one side would be of short duration, and only through such a high level of preparedness is it possible to discourage the opponent of the notion that an attack might be profitable. Napoleon's famous dictum that it is not possible to sit on bayonets seems to have lost its validity in the nuclear age.

The Nature of Coexistence

The Soviet Union has clearly acknowledged the competitive character of present international relations. What is rather engagingly called "peaceful coexistence" signifies to Soviet leaders the repudiation of war for solving disputes, respect for the territorial integrity and sovereignty of all states, noninterference in other countries' internal affairs, and acknowledgment of equality in the political and economic relations of states. It clearly does not imply the cessation of competition.[7] Coexistence is war without warfare. Soviet thinking certainly does not equate coexistence with acceptance of a static condition. In fact, brushfire wars and wars by proxy are permissible methods even though the superpowers conduct their mutual relations with the instruments of political rather than military warfare.

This view is better attuned to the realities of the cold war than a formula equating coexistence with cooperation, a view that gained wide popularity in the United States in the early days of proclaimed coexistence. However, "peaceful coexistence" should not be dismissed as a mere cloak for psychopolitical warfare. It represents real progress in international relations even if there still is no room for bucolic contentment. If peaceful coexistence has accomplished nothing else, it has created a state of mind that is prepared to tolerate the opponent's distasteful ideology and institutional order. The probability of disaster, into which zealots and bunglers might otherwise plunge the world, has thereby been greatly reduced.

In the course of time, the nature of the cold war has undergone significant changes reflecting the changed relations between the superpowers. The cold war is no longer a simple contest between two fairly closed blocs in fierce competition with each other. The gigantic struggle along clearly drawn fronts has resolved itself into a series of contests, diverse in type and diffuse in location. Cold war tactics not only show considerable variety but are adapted to local situations to such a degree that racial conflicts and the quest for economic improvement appear to dwarf the bipolar contest. Further changes have occurred superseding, or in any event obscuring, the earlier cold war pattern. The emergence of common interests of the United States and the Soviet Union has already been mentioned. In addition, China has arisen as the chief cold war opponent of the United States. Not only does it seem, at times, that the Russo-American cold war has been superseded by the Sino-American cold war, but it also seems that frequently Soviet sympathies are on the American rather than on the Chinese side.

The Chinese have openly charged the Russians with being American sympathizers, and not without cause. The tone of cold war strategy has become unmistakably more moderate on both Russian and American sides. The Soviet Union has shown little sympathy for the belligerency advocated by the Chinese. Both superpowers have, generally, respected each other's spheres of influence and have avoided the kind of policy that would help more bellicose factions seize power in the other's country. In fact, in the interest of furthering the *détente,* the United States in 1962 and 1963 sold large amounts of wheat to the Soviet Union and Soviet bloc countries. The policy was severely criticized at home and abroad. It was charged that the United States was giving the Soviet Union something for nothing, thereby helping the enemy save face. The sales actually made good sense politically. The United States is more interested in the continuation of the domestic status quo in the Soviet Union than in gaining a temporary advantage in the psychological cold war.

All these are hopeful signs, but they do not signal the end of the Russo-American cold war or assure the durability of coexistence. President Johnson's appeal to the Soviet Union for a common understanding of the two countries and the renunciation of the cold war was rebuffed.[8] While the equal destructive capabilities of the two powers are cause for hope that coexistence will continue, unless one or both of the antagonists loses its head, sensitivity to change continues and the possibility of resort to violence is heightened by the extraordinary striking power at their disposal.

To evaluate the cold war changes realistically, it must first of all be observed that the displacement of the Soviet Union by China as the cold war antagonist of the United States is more apparent than real. The Sino-American cold war is different in quality because China's role lacks the plausibility that can only be given by the backing of an effective military force. This is amply demonstrated by the American participation in the Vietnamese war. The United States would have been far more reluctant to become involved if Vietnam were within the primary security sphere of the Soviet Union. While promises of support to the North Vietnamese have been far from unambiguous, China reportedly has made clear that it "has no intention of provoking a war with the United States."[9]

Any idea that the Russo-American cold war has been terminated disregards the continuation of fears and tension.

Although the present distribution of power justifies the hope that ultimate disaster may be avoided, there is no reason to assume that this will resolve political conflicts. Even if neither of the Big Two is aiming at more than a satisfactory measure of security, this alone cannot remove prevailing fears, and there remains a strong feeling that somewhere a stand must be taken against the advance of hostile forces. It may, therefore, be expected that the politics of peaceful coexistence will continue to reflect the tensions of the cold war. There is little hope in the near future for disarmament, termination of military service, and reduced defense budgets. The most that can be expected is that a military clash will be avoided and that the present equilibrium of political and military power will be maintained even if this involves the risk of heightened tensions. Since no settlement seems possible, it would be imprudent for either the United States or the Soviet Union unilaterally to call off the cold war, if for no other reason than that the cost in terms of lost friends and allies would be too heavy to sustain. The Soviet position was made clear by Chairman Khrushchev when he reaffirmed his commitment to peaceful coexistence as "the only sensible policy in the age of rocket-nuclear weapons," but simultaneously promised military help to Cuba, China, North Vietnam, North Korea, and East Germany in the event of invasion.[10]

The sporadic relaxations of cold war tensions furnish no reason to hail the beginning of a new era relegating the cold war to the past. The most hopeful development was the limited nuclear test ban treaty of 1963 between the United States and the Soviet Union. Further conciliatory moves were made by the United States. President Kennedy committed himself to relaxing cold war tensions, declared his willingness to liquidate American strategic bases in Turkey, and agreed to sell surplus wheat to the Soviet Union. All these were encouraging signs, but on closer inspection such pacific gestures turned out be less meaningful. The liquidation of American bases in Turkey would have little practical significance since American striking force has been transferred to mobile and maritime bases. The test ban treaty, too, was a more modest achievement than was generally assumed. It has neither pacified international relations nor reduced military competition in other than nuclear areas; even in the realm of nuclear technology it has failed to ensure stability.

Although it is true, as observed earlier, that the area of common interests has widened and the avoidance of all-out war has become the overriding concern of both superpowers, there remains too much of an overlap of vital interests to permit genuine pacification. The leaders of both camps have consistently accompanied their peaceful gestures with stern warnings. President Kennedy assured Americans of his determination to maintain the nation's strength unimpaired, since major tensions would remain as a result of the two countries' "wholly different concepts of the world, its freedom, its future." [11] Chairman Khrushchev expressed equal determination to step up the defenses of the Soviet Union.[12] Thus, the objectives of the two opponents appear to have remained unchanged.

The record shows that the two leaders were not indulging in empty rhetoric. Since the signing of the test ban treaty, tensions have not been relaxed in Berlin, in Laos, or in Vietnam. Political rivalry between the Big Two continues in Africa, Asia, Latin America, and the Middle East. The Vietnamese situation is of particular interest. The Soviet government has persisted in denouncing American imperialism in the Vietnamese War. These denunciations have not been tempered by a common hostility toward China, which in many respects has brought the United States and the Soviet Union closer together. The Soviet Union has, in fact, no intention of letting the hegemony over Southeast Asia fall to China, and is bent on wresting from the Chinese the championship of the communist cause in that area. Although denunciations of American imperialism and the aid given to North Vietnam are directed more against China than against the United States, the Soviet Union must follow an anti-American course, and it must do so with all the sincerity necessary to make its anti-American policy convincing. The natural result has been growing tensions between the United States and the Soviet Union, which are seriously threatening the tacit accommodation that prevailed prior to the overt American participation in Vietnam. In fact, it seems possible that a further extension of the American war against North Vietnam might bring not only China but also the Soviet Union into the conflict.

The Middle East is another area in which superpower competition has remained unabated. The Soviet Union has tried to build up the Arab states through material aid and moral encouragement to a degree that would enable them to eradicate the remnants of Western influence and control. The defeat of the Arab states in the Arab-Israeli war of June 1967 once again ominously heightened tensions between the United States and the Soviet Union as the latter endeavored to recoup in the political arena the losses suffered on the field of battle.

Despite the superpowers' common interest in coexistence, the pattern of their mutual relations remains militant and competitive. The rather sharp anti-American line adopted in 1966 by the Twenty-third Congress of the Communist Party of the Soviet Union does not necessarily signal the end of coexistence policy, but it reflects the practical political pressures confronting the Soviet Union. Sustained influence on Allied and friendly uncommitted nations requires a firm ideological and political position. The challenge of Communist China limits the scope of compromises with the United States. Much of the continuing tension results from the frequent inability of the superpowers to curb their allies. The adventurism of the Arab states in the summer of 1967 sparked off a crisis in Soviet-American relations that the Soviet Union could not have cleared away even in its most conciliatory moments in view of the *fait accompli* created by its friends. The United States has also been repeatedly saddled with liabilities emanating from its allies; Nationalist China and South Vietnam are cases in point. And Allied resistance was a stumbling block in United States efforts to negotiate a nuclear nonproliferation agreement with the Soviet Union.

Another problem which has hampered Soviet-American accommodation is the steady increase in armaments on both sides. The need felt by one side to correct a moderate military imbalance may easily produce a major disturbance.

The efforts of the Soviet Union to close the missile gap of the early 1960's has spurred the United States to revise its nuclear and missile technology and to give serious consideration to the development of a costly antimissile defense system to match the advances made by the Soviet Union.

Although annoyances, recriminations, and suspicions persist, the striving for accommodation remains strong even in the midst of clashes in Vietnam and the Middle East. Cooperation between the superpowers has been widened in the cultural and diplomatic areas as well as in the exploration of outer space, and, most encouragingly, in the negotiation of a nuclear nonproliferation treaty. There has been a growing tendency toward cautious probing of the issues and a willingness to substitute diplomatic maneuvers for open defiance. Even at the height of the Middle Eastern crisis, the Soviet Union refrained from challenging the United States through military intervention on behalf of the Arab states and, while bitterly denouncing the United States in the United Nations General Assembly, consented to a summit meeting at Glassboro between President Johnson and Premier Kosygin in late June, 1967. Yet it is necessary to guard against mistaking a cautious pursuit for an end to the cold war. Not only is there no basis for relaxing vigilance on either side, but continued vigilance is a requisite for preserving the gains that have been made.

CHAPTER FOUR

COLD WAR STRATEGY AND POLITICS

ARMAMENTS

The cold war differs from all-out military war chiefly in its methods. This is not to say that military matters have ceased to be relevant. The dependence of coexistence on an equilibrium of destructive capabilities quite naturally has kept alive a keen interest in the problems of armaments and military strategy. Evidently, war has not been banished from the earth, local wars continue with considerable abandon, and are fought with great intensity and anxiously watched, if not supported, by the superpowers. The important change is the relations between the United States and the Soviet Union. Both are assiduously trying to avoid a military clash. In their relations, actual force has been displaced by threats of force, which neither those issuing the threat nor those threatened expect to result in war. The war threats of the Soviet Union against the American blockade of Cuba no doubt produced some anxiety in Washington, but they were not seriously expected to materialize. Not all situations can be met with similar assurance, and the possibility that coexistence may terminate and the cold war be transformed into a hot war cannot be dismissed. A comparable

American action within the Soviet orbit very likely would evoke a different reaction. The occasion may also arise that the big powers have so deeply committed themselves as to have closed all escapes.

Despite the ever-present danger of war, the contest between the two worlds is centered in the non-military arena. Notwithstanding their mutual distrust, competition, and belligerent frames of mind, both the United States and the Soviet Union prefer the status quo to a change in the international distribution of power that involves the risk of their lands being devastated. This does not mean that they have agreed to preserve rigidly all existing conditions or to prevent any changes from taking place. The Soviet Union in particular, for reasons of power and ideology, continually stirs up ferment as far as overall political interests permit. Even in paying lip service to the protection of the status quo, Soviet leaders do not seem prepared to bring the social and economic revolutions in Asia and Africa to a halt. Khrushchev made this quite clear when he insisted that the status quo was "not the preservation of existing boundaries and balances." [1] However, there is no actual indication that the Soviet Union is any more inclined than the United States to risk total destruction. Both nations are sufficiently content with their world position to prefer the present distribution of power to hazardous adventures. [2] The Soviet Union, in fact, has shown little patience with allies or sympathizers who endeavor to break up the bipolar system, as the acrimonious debate with China over proper communist strategy reveals. It has unequivocally rejected the Chinese advocacy of a more aggressive line.

These considerations explain why the Big Two have plunged into the armaments race with great vigor and are willing to make expenditures of unprecedented proportions for nuclear and rocket weapons at a time when neither expects to put them to actual use. Even though it appears unlikely that either side will attack as soon as it believes it can do so without suffering massive retaliation, prudence requires each to assume that the opponent might attack if not adequately deterred by calculation of the consequences. Self-interested calculation, therefore, makes it necessary for both sides to keep up with the opponent's technological advances and to build a plausible machine of massive retaliation to continue the futility of attack. The psychological effect of this knowledge is important. The military role in the cold war has been well stated by Madariaga: "We must prepare for a hot war to keep the war cold," [3] and by Churchill: "We arm to parley." The principles of cold war can, then, be reduced to talking loudly and carrying a big stick without expecting to use it. The big stick being waved by the Soviet Union is the recurrent, impressive displays of its most recent weapons, which are helpful in keeping allies in line, making the uncommitted receptive to political overtures, and instilling fear in the opponent. The policy of the big stick also seems to be the chief rationale behind the Russo-American space race. It is not apparent whether stations on the moon or on Mars would be of any practical value, peaceful or military; but it is politically important to keep abreast of the opponent's scientific and engineering accomplishments.

The stability of the present condition seems greatly enhanced by the uncertainty surrounding nuclear and missile technology and the unpredictability of the consequences if these weapons were released. Therefore, the chances of another world war are appreciably reduced under bipolar conditions as compared with the traditional multiple balance of power.

THE POLITICAL WEAPON

The tacit "antisuicide pact" does not permit the superpowers to rest on their laurels and banish all expansionist thought from their minds. It is unlikely that their quest for security can be satisfied by a static policy. Persistent efforts to forge ahead of the competitor seem better attuned to the needs of an insecure state of mind. But dynamic policies will eventually produce military clashes that, however limited and geographically remote, harbor potential for escalation to a general nuclear war. The Big Two, therefore, have been generally reluctant to intercede militarily in local wars, and when they have done so, their participation has

usually been indirect and limited in scope. When one of
the superpowers has become directly involved in a local
war, as the United States is in Vietnam, both sides have
endeavored to prevent the war from spreading and developing into a full-fledged nuclear war. The American decision
to participate was made with considerable reluctance and
was prompted by a fear of the effects of a communist
victory in Vietnam. Soviet response to the American belligerency has been slow, deliberate, and restrained. It has
been limited to moral and diplomatic support of North
Vietnam, censure of the United States, and material aid on
a limited scale.

Instead of military intervention, both superpowers normally promote their causes through less direct means. The
Soviet Union, for example, openly offers weapons to "any
people fighting against oppression." [4] The United States,
too, prefers indirect means, where possible, of meeting the
communist challenge head-on. For example, permission was
granted Germany to transfer to Israel tanks purchased in
the United States, to counteract Soviet arms shipments to
Arab countries.[5] Only when the Germans withdrew from
the arrangement because of Arab pressures did the United
States assume delivery to Israel to preserve the balance of
power in the Middle East.[6]

It has become increasingly fashionable to encourage wars
by proxy fought by satellites or "volunteers," or, better still,
to let international war take the form of national revolution
or civil war. The most recent cold war method is communist revolution incognito used in countries where pro-
communist sentiments are not overwhelming. Castro's revolution in Cuba is the classic example. Regardless of whether
Fidel Castro embraced communism before or after the
revolution, what started out as an indigenous uprising
against a corrupt government ended up in putting the
country firmly in the communist camp after the revolution
was brought to a successful conclusion. Such indirect
methods of warfare lend themselves to the superpowers.

The aversion of the Big Two against direct military involvements and their success in avoiding them has not
relegated military considerations to insignificance. Although

control over territories is not as vital to the nuclear powers as it was in the days of conventional warfare, territorial competition continues undiminished. Since the United States still professes to check Soviet extension of direct territorial control, as well as the extension of political control through instigation of communist revolutions, conventional military strategy remains a matter of concern. Preparedness in conventional terms also has the decided advantage of permitting the Big Two to contain hostile forces without resorting to all-out nuclear and missile warfare. In the cold war, however, military considerations are subordinate and supplementary to political considerations. In fact, political and military spheres are not always separable since the efficacy of political weapons frequently depends on the availability of up-to-date military arms. In general, cold war battles are political battles, and the task of winning followers through ideological conversion has a high priority.

The attempts of the superpowers at political consolidation mainly follow three lines: first, to draw their allies together into a working unit; second, to win new allies; and third, to encourage and strengthen the resistance of the uncommitted to the influence of the opposing bloc. To accomplish these ends, propaganda and political maneuver are continually gaining importance as strategic weapons. In part, cold war politics are carried on in the United Nations. The world organization provides an arena for political maneuvers, propaganda, mutual recrimination, and pacification. However, the keenest competition between the contestants occurs outside the United Nations framework. The United States carries on its propaganda war chiefly through the Voice of America and an extensive system of information agencies. The Soviet Union relies more on subversion and indoctrination via local communist parties. An especially fertile field for Soviet propaganda is former colonial areas, and every shred of native resentment against the West is systematically exploited. It is in the newly rising states that the Soviet Union tends to find the most receptive audience for its political propaganda. Soviet advances in Far Eastern countries are particularly effective through the fusion of nationalism and communism. Despite the conceptual contradiction between communist internationalism and the extreme nationalism of the emergent countries, the Soviet Union has managed with great skill to adapt communist doctrine to local preferences.

The propaganda war, consisting largely of mutual recriminations over the oppression of other peoples, has stimulated the employment of a number of political gambits. One of the more favored and effective methods of the Soviet Union has been recurrent peace offensives. By proposing a palpably unworkable plan to stabilize peace through the settlement of the major outstanding issues, it has repeatedly forced the United States into the awkward position of rejecting as impractical schemes designed to arouse mankind's hopes for a secure future. This strategy was, very likely, responsible for the crises over Berlin and Cuba. After driving the United States to the brink of war, the Soviet Union has repeatedly revealed itself to the world in the role of a savior, who at the last minute has averted war through generous concessions to appease the American "war-mongers." Such seemingly noble endeavors, accompanied as they are by much fanfare and a deluge of pious protestations effectively obscuring the origins of the crisis, cannot fail to create a favorable image among a peace-hungry humanity. At the same time, the Soviet Union must be careful not to let the image become too peaceable, and thus it has occasionally given a formidable display of its destructive capabilities. This technique was used dramatically in the fall of 1961 to terminate a nuclear moratorium by setting off atomic explosions of unprecedented and terrifying proportions. The purpose, no doubt, was political rather than military and was aimed less at the United States than at the rest of the world. The Soviet Union apparently expected that this would have an especially salutary effect upon its allies, who are highly susceptible to this type of intimidation.

A particularly ingenious variant of the peace offensive has been the call for summit conferences. The expectation that Russo-American tensions can be relaxed by settling all outstanding issues seems futile since neither side is willing to yield on anything of substance. Therefore, the call to the summit has never been reassuring. Statesmen evidently are aware of the futility of attempts to explore possibilities of an overall settlement when they publicly commit themselves in advance not to yield to pressure and thereby remove the very rationale of negotiation. Although such pronouncements are undoubtedly intended as publicity stunts, they make a valid point. The basic issues dividing the United States and the Soviet Union are not the negotiable kind. Surely, fear and suspicion can neither be reduced to debatable terms nor be talked out of existence. The necessary vagueness of cold war goals would seem to render negotiations pointless. American leaders are usually aware of this melancholy circumstance and are reluctant to agree to such meetings. They attend, however, when Soviet pressure can no longer be evaded. At these times, despite optimistic expectations harbored in many quarters, the prediction could have been made that no tangible achievements would result.

The Soviet strategy of alternating crises and peace offensives evidently was designed to test the American determination to hold the line, to undermine American alliances, and to put the world under a debt of gratitude to the Soviet Union. The challenge of such a strategy cannot be met; it can only be anticipated by equally aggressive maneuvers. Faced with such diplomatic assaults, American policy has been handicapped by its defensive nature. The Rapacki Plan, presented to the United Nations in 1957, calling for nuclear disarmament and the neutralization of East Germany, West Germany, Poland, and Czechoslovakia is a good illustration. Suspecting that the chief purpose of the plan was to weaken NATO by arousing unfounded hopes for eventual disengagement, the United States was again forced into the unrewarding position of shattering the hopes of a panic-stricken world for the peaceful life so generously offered by the Soviets. In 1965, the United States belatedly resorted to the peace offensive to settle the conflict in Vietnam. If it was intended to discredit the Soviet Union, the attack miscarried. At that time, the Soviet Union was engaged in mediating between India and Pakistan. These efforts were well received in Asia and were designed to create the image of the Soviet Union as the power of peace while the United

States and China were involved in the war in Vietnam.[7] To
be sure, the Soviet strategy has not been unequivocally
successful. Its many vacillations have tended to strengthen
the unity of the anticommunist alliance. However, such
reverses cannot obscure the advantage the Soviet Union
has derived from taking the initiative or from the paralyzing
effect of the negative policy of containment through which
the United States has tried to defend its position.

The circumstances, then, leave little room for optimism
concerning the possible accomplishments of summit conferences. Moreover, the pursuit of a grand design as such
is not without danger. If undertaken in good faith, it may
cause a relaxation of military preparedness at home and a
split in the alliance systems abroad. An even more dangerous by-product is the possibility of a crusading spirit in the
anticommunist camp, brought about by defeat and disappointed hopes, that could precipitate war—another war to
end all wars. Summit conferences, at best, are an opiate
of short effect. More frequently, they are a cold war weapon
rather than a means of negotiating a settlement. In fact,
they are a sure-fire weapon if used offensively since the
user sets the terms. Whenever Washington reacted to Soviet
proposals with understandable reluctance, it also suffered
setbacks in the battle for peoples' minds. This is not to say
that conferences are generally useless or dangerous. There
is a distinction between summit conferences called to settle
all outstanding issues and conferences called for the *ad hoc*
settlement of defined or definable issues. The latter type is
not only possible but necessary. It is not a venture into the
realm of utopia but a concrete attempt by diplomatic crafts-
men to remove causes of conflict. To refuse to agree to talks
of this nature would be tantamount to breaking off all con-
tact and might, indeed, have disastrous consequences.

Recurrent attempts to devise schemes for disarmament or
arms control are of more interest as cold war weapons than
because of their intrinsic merit. In view of the catastrophic
prospects of a nuclear-missile war, it is not surprising that
such endeavors persist with extraordinary stubbornness. The
demolition of the implements of destruction alone would
seem to give adequate assurances against global disaster.

However, the results thus far have been discouraging. Such concrete accomplishments as the agreement not to put nuclear weapons into orbit and the limited nuclear test ban treaty have not reduced the destructive capabilities of the two nuclear powers. Nor is it likely in the near future that a mutually acceptable formula will be worked out that could provide a basis for real disarmament or arms control and also satisfy the security needs of both sides.

It is not difficult to see that disarmament conferences can be useful propaganda devices through which responsibility for continued international tension can be shifted to the opponent.[8] Although over a period of time, the propaganda advantages have not all been on one side, the United States has more often been handicapped by the seriousness of its search for workable solutions and the cautiousness with which it has consequently proceeded. Hesitancy is usually ill rewarded in a propaganda war, and Soviet leaders have been quick to brand American caution as "monstrous" in the face of the danger of nuclear mass destruction. In contrast, the Russians have piously proclaimed their own readiness to eliminate the present threat to human survival.

THE ECONOMIC WEAPON

Political strategies, no doubt, are well adapted to the cold war. But they would be of questionable effectiveness in the long run if unaccompanied by concrete prospects of material improvement. The United States quickly recognized the need for complementary economic strategies. Shortly after the commencement of the cold war, it devised bold, imaginative programs of economic aid to countries whose depressed economies rendered them vulnerable to communist penetration and of military aid to those willing but militarily unable to fight off communist assaults.

The first step was the program developed in 1947 to extend military and economic aid to Greece and Turkey. Initially these were stop-gap measures to strengthen the resistance of the former country to domestic communist forces and of the latter to the pressures of the Soviet Union to surrender bases in the Dardanelles after the withdrawal

of British forces from Greece. These *ad hoc* measures were
accompanied by a general policy declaration by President
Truman that held out the promise of support to other
peoples "resisting attempted subjugation by armed minorities or by outside pressures." The announcement was
quickly followed by the Marshall Plan, providing economic
aid to the hard-pressed European countries to help restore
their war-torn economies. It was expected that restored
economies could stop the communist wave threatening
Western Europe. The plan was so successful that the United
States applied the same formula to impoverished underdeveloped countries. The vulnerability of such countries to
communist assaults was to be diminished by demonstrating
that other than communist means were available to raise
their standard of living. Within a few years, the emphasis
shifted from economic to military aid as it became apparent
that local wars would continue. Over the entire period
since the inception of foreign aid programs, the largest
amounts have been allocated to economic purposes and
about half of that total to defense assistance, although the
distribution has not been consistent from year to year.
There have been years when military aid has topped the
list. Both forms of aid have been supplemented by technical
assistance programs to help the new economically underdeveloped nation become integrated into the modern industrial world.

Despite the predominance of economic aid and the persistent concern with the economic soundness of the grants
made on the part of the American administering agencies,
political and security objectives undeniably had top priority.
Although the ideal of a universal security system perhaps
was never wholly excluded from American thinking, the
measures taken complemented and supported the policy of
containment. Formal diplomatic consolidation was not
enough to contain communist power. If the alliances concluded for that purpose were to be of any practical value,
members had to have internal political stability and a sufficiently high level of military preparedness to contribute
their fair share to the common defense. Both political stability and military preparedness depended, to a large extent,

on the soundness of their economic orders. To close the lines of containment it was also desirable to extend anti-communist resistance into the more remote parts of the world. The Point Four Program was the first step, providing aid for economic and industrial advances of underdeveloped areas. The rising expectations of backward peoples for economic development—aroused by the Atlantic Charter and other promises of the Allies during the war—made such aid imperative lest the disappointed turn to communism for the realization of their aspirations. Economic and industrial development aid eventually became an integral part of the overall foreign aid program of the United States.

A further step forward was the conception of the Alliance for Progress as a comprehensive development plan for Latin America inspired and, to a large extent, supported by the United States. The scheme went considerably beyond earlier aid programs. The extension of economic aid to Europe rested on the assumption that the economies of recipient countries would be rebuilt and this in turn would enhance political stability. Aid to backward countries was largely designed to support anticommunist governments and to strengthen the friendliness of their people toward the United States. It was, however, becoming increasingly clear that the latter goal was attainable in countries outside the orbit of Western political standards and experience only if an equitable distribution of economic benefits could be ensured. If a program was to be effective, it was necessary to combine economic aid with social and political reforms, since aid to unreconstructed feudal systems could not be expected to produce stability in an era of rising popular expectations, or to elicit much popular sympathy for the United States. The program combined economic reform under democratic rule with American aid. By reducing poverty and illiteracy, it was hoped that stability and progress could be promoted. Aid, therefore, was made contingent on internal social and political reforms to provide more equitable distribution of land and of tax burdens. Such changes were intended to create a favorable climate for democratic development and to build up immunities

against pressures from the Right and the Far Left. President
Johnson, to convey the seriousnes of the American commit
ment to hemispheric solidarity, went so far as to identify
the objectives of the alliance with those of his Great So
ciety.[9]

The American aid program to underdeveloped countries
represented a challenge that the Soviet Union had to meet
It was not willing to stand by idly while uncommitted coun
tries were drifting into the American camp as a result o
their economic dependence on the United States. It wa
important to present alternatives to the Western programs
Even if it was not possible to draw recipients into th
Soviet bloc, closer political ties could be established and
perhaps, *ad hoc* support of specific Soviet policies secured
In any event, the emancipation of such areas from Ameri
can tutelage, which could be expected to result, would be
worthwhile gain. The containment of the Soviet Unio
would not become an encirclement. A further inducemen
to follow the American example was provided by the nee
to preserve political equilibrium. To maintain Soviet inter
national prestige on a level with the United States, it wa
not enough to step up the production of consumer goods a
home and to bring Soviet military preparations up to pa
The real test was to do all this and still be able to provid
other nations with some of the things they wanted.

In 1954 the world witnessed the beginnings of a foreig
aid program emanating from the communist bloc. By 195
the program was fully developed, and it has continued t
progress. The official view of the Soviet government look
upon economics as the ultimate criterion of communi
superiority over capitalism and considers revolutionary sl
gans devoid of economic content as futile.[10] Even mor
revealing is the willingness of the Soviet Union to abando
its initial objections to and participate in a United Natio
project to set up an Asian development bank. The need
build up prestige in an area where its position is challenge
by the United States and China evidently has impelled th
Soviet government to overcome its dislike for a proje
initiated and promoted by the United States.[11]

The Soviet foreign aid program has covered a wide range of activities including financial aid and grants, arms deals, and barter agreements,[12] and has extended to the Arab world, South and Southeast Asia, Africa, and, finally Latin America. Major emphasis has been placed on the newly rising states of Africa. The communist countries of Eastern Europe have been made to participate in the program as donors rather than as recipients. The Soviet Union has preferred to extend its aid in the form of credits at low interest rates to making outright grants in order to give its program a businesslike appearance. Most of the assistance has been given for economic and technical purposes; only a little over one-fifth of the total has been military aid. The preconditions for obtaining aid have been generally flexible, with political expediency rather than economic soundness being the criterion. The terms of repayment have also been flexible. In particular, the Soviet Union has been willing to accept commodities or local currency as far as possible.

PROBLEMS OF COLD WAR DIPLOMACY

The cold war battle for the minds of men requires extraordinary skill and flexibility. These requirements are not easily met. One of the chief factors that has hampered cold war diplomacy is the rigidity that characterizes political thinking under bipolar conditions. By and large, the Soviet Union has been more adept in employing political weapons, whereas the United States has been more successful in areas of technical assistance. In particular, the Soviet Union has been skillful in coordinating military activities with propaganda by alternately displaying its reasonableness and its enormous destructive power. This demonstration has been calculated to produce favorable reactions on the part of the uncommitted countries. The Soviet Union has missed no opportunity to kindle hatred of Western colonialism and to hold out the promise of communist salvation as a natural sequel to liberation. In relation to nations allied with the United States, the Soviet Union has employed more subtle methods. Through an expansive display of reasonableness, it has tried to remove the unifying core of the United States' defensive alliances, while sowing disunity and exploiting disagreement wherever possible. Within its own bloc, a combination of indoctrination and fear inspired by the proximity of the Red Army have been relied upon to achieve its political goals.

Soviet Problems

Soviet strategies have not been uniformly successful. The economic weapon, at best, has produced temporary results. It has not succeeded in securing lasting Soviet influence in any country outside the Soviet orbit to which the Soviet Union has extended aid or with which it has traded. Slow delivery and the low quality of Soviet goods have created an unfavorable atmosphere. In the political sphere, Soviet strategies have had varying success. They have frequently proved effective in the area of the most intense big power competition—the uncommitted countries of Africa and Asia, which for various reasons tend to be attracted to communism. By contrast, attempts to drive a wedge between the United States and its allies have been frustrated by the recurrent inability to follow a policy consistent with its overall strategy. Considerations of domestic and intrabloc politics have, from time to time, required a display of aggressiveness toward the noncommunist world that has strengthened the solidarity of the opposing bloc. Soviet diplomacy has probably encountered its most vexatious problems within the Soviet bloc proper. The defection of Yugoslavia in the late 1940's caused great embarrassment, and even after many years of alternating threats and attempts at persuasion Yugoslavia is not securely back in the Soviet fold. Nationalist revolts have challenged Soviet control in Hungary, Poland, and East Germany. Although the Soviet Union has prevented the defection of these countries through brute force, its political position in the world-at-large has suffered as a result of such episodes.

The most serious problem, no doubt, has been the split with China, which has challenged not only the Kremlin's infallibility in ideological matters but also its political leadership in the communist world. The difficulties of the Soviet Union in Southeast Asia have been aggravated by attempts to exploit anti-American resentments of non-communist as well as communist populist forces. The call for "democratic" unity against "American imperialism" [13] has necessitated the support of noncommunist governments. Such collaboration has worked as long as a *modus vivendi* could be found between governments and local communist parties. But whenever it has become necessary for non-communist governments to crack down on local communists, the Soviet Union has suffered serious strategic setbacks.

The failures of Soviet strategy can only in part be explained by diplomatic bungling. They must be attributed to more basic reasons. One of the most severe handicaps of Soviet policy has been communist ideological fixations. Although since the end of the Second World War the Soviet Union has succeeded remarkably well in adapting Marxism to the unexpected persistence of nationalism, there has remained a tendency to underestimate the vitality of nationalism as an *idée force*. Thus, Soviet efforts to impose the Bolshevik pattern of organization upon indigenous communist parties has provoked great hostility within the international communist movement. Further difficulties have arisen from the need to establish an order of priority in political matters. For example, the Soviet Union has repeatedly stirred up the Berlin issue, perhaps against its better judgment, to placate resentments at home or within its bloc even if it was thereby promoting solidarity of the Western alliance. However, the greatest Soviet liability has been the unalluring picture presented by communism wherever it has seized control of government. Communism has its greatest appeal when proposed as a method to alleviate existing national problems; in practice, its methods of governing usually evoke resentment. The peoples of Western and Central Europe, particularly after almost half a century of communist rule, find the ways of communism both alien and distasteful.

American Problems

The United States has been confronted with similar difficulties. The dissensions within its camp have, perhaps, been less dramatic and less bitter than those plaguing the Soviet Union, but the resurgence of nationalism in Europe has substantially reduced American influence there. But the greatest disappointment, undoubtedly, has been the ineffectiveness of the economic weapon in winning the friendship of the newly rising states to an extent commensurate with American efforts and investments. Attempts to secure the Asian fringes as allies against communist penetration have not succeeded. Although the United States, inspired by the success of NATO in Europe, managed to build an Asian alliance, the area has not been effectively integrated into its defense system. The region that has been least accessible to American influence has been the Middle East, since the Suez crisis. The most that economic relations have accomplished in a majority of Middle-Eastern countries has been to reduce hostility rather than to win friendship.

The chief handicap of American policy has been the defensive nature of its overall strategy and of its tactical situation in specific crisis areas—in Europe, Latin America, Asia, and Africa. That this state of affairs is less the result of choice than of the role that has fallen to the United States in the bipolar contest makes the predicament all the more serious. The maintenance of the status quo has limited the United States to the modest role of guardian of individual rights and container of Soviet expansionism. In a radically changing world, this is not a rewarding task. The conservatism inherent in a defensive position has prevented new ideas of sufficient force to parry the ideological thrusts of the communists. The support of bankrupt regimes, or of the constitutional orders within which such regimes are operating, is hardly apt to inspire those determined to build a new world. Against the devotion to so grandiose a task, military force and economic aid administered through routine channels can, at best, be temporarily successful in suppressing or preventing revolutions.

Military methods have been of little value in the long run where the bipolar contest has taken the form of civil strife between communist and anticommunist forces. The war in Vietnam clearly shows that revolutionary movements brought about by deeply felt popular resentments or disappointments are difficult to suppress, and it may ultimately prove the futility of military means when employed against subversive organizations rather than against national armies. This type of warfare transcends the military arena and is aimed at cultural, ideological, political, and economic spheres. Although, by making an all-out effort, the United States could very likely win a military victory over North Vietnam, it seems unlikely that the United States will have accomplished its purpose by bringing operations there to a successful conclusion. Cessation of hostilities on American terms will not mark the end of communist infiltration, and it will not bring stability to Southeast Asia.

The economic weapon, which has been the main focus of American efforts, has been far more successful than the military approach. Economic aid programs, in fact, are a necessity if the United States wants to bridge the gap between its unique standard of living and that of the rest of the world. Refusal to share its abundance could only lead to complete alienation from humanity.[14] However, the generous American economic aid programs have been marred by two basic flaws: one inherent in American thinking, the other in the very conditions that the program was to correct. The United States assumed that economic improvement would by itself generate political stability. This assumption has not been borne out by experience. Aid given to unpopular governments has been far from reassuring to the rising masses in Latin America, Asia, and Africa, and has done little to placate their anxieties. Moreover, the presumed straight-line connection between economic and political stability has made economic soundness of proposed development projects the main criterion of American support. This procedure has enabled the communists in many places to charge the United States with intervention. It has also been a source of frustration to the recipient governments who have valued investment in prestige items more highly than funds to satisfy basic necessities. By contrast, the opportunistic aid program of the Soviet Union has often been more successful. Being more interested in fostering instability in areas having noncommunist governments, it has tended to extend aid for any desired purpose regardless of merit.

The American aid program could perhaps be easily corrected. A more serious problem, however, is the unsettling and undesired effect that rapid industrialization has had upon underdeveloped societies. Not only does a sudden changeover to an industrial economy dislocate workers and create at least temporary unemployment, it also tends to uproot people deeply attached to their folkways. Sudden social change puts severe strains even on stable societies. It can be expected to disrupt completely traditional relationships and customs of unstable and backward societies. The dissolution of the social and political consensus and the need for economic planning create an atmosphere favorable to an authoritarian government rather than a democratic one. To make things worse, capitalistic methods have aroused suspicion and outright hostility in their own right. The record of capitalism overseas has not been good. It has perpetuated corrupt, oppressive governments and has often delayed modernization. Now that many areas have obtained political independence, it is feared that economic aid will in effect continue to support these same ruling groups. Moreover, the slowness of economic progress has created a considerable impatience with existing governments and those supporting them.

People in poor countries can, therefore, be easily persuaded to try new governments and new methods. They have little confidence that rapid economic progress can be attained and maintained through democratic organization. The impressive achievements of the Soviet Union within less than half a century, whatever their actual economic foundations, present a most inspiring example. The often reckless promises of the Soviet Union to provide methods that will bring instant improvement of present conditions strengthen the appeal of communism even further. Regardless of the ultimate consequences, this approach gives the

Soviet Union an immediate tactical advantage in its conquest of the underdeveloped world. The absence of traditions on which to rest either industrialism or communism has been no serious obstacle in the way of Soviet strategy. Its claim is revolutionary, and revolution is what the masses want. It satisfies the needs and desires of the moment without regard to economic soundness or ultimate consequences. The Soviet Union has effectively demonstrated that it can topple an archaic and corrupt political system and industrialize a backward country in a hurry. It offers experience in state enterprise where private initiative is inadequate to cope with economic and industrial problems. This is not to say that all is well on the Soviet side. The rate of growth in the Soviet Union has fallen short of expectations. The Soviet alliance is in disarray. Eastern Europe is far from reliable, and China is challenging Soviet leadership of the communist world. Soviet economic aid to uncommitted countries has severely strained the Soviet economy, frequently without producing the desired political results. Tough commercial policies and the inferiority of Soviet goods have caused much resentment abroad. All this may be comforting to the United States, but it provides no basis for complacency.

A good illustration of the American attempt to improve its image is the Alliance for Progress. President Kennedy resolved to make aid contingent upon social and political reforms so that its benefits would trickle down to the lower social strata. In this way it was hoped that the United States would be looked upon as a liberator rather than an imperialist. Yet within two years, it appeared that the statesmanlike project had failed to produce the anticipated results. Although economic progress has slowly been made, particularly in the areas of tax and land reforms, benefits derived by the various countries have been uneven. In many areas, expectations were raised beyond attainable levels, and the resulting impatience has added to the already existing ferment. Moreover, the social reforms initiated in accordance with the terms of the alliance, have increased political tensions and in many countries have fostered political instability. In its desire to maintain stability, the

United States let itself become involved in arming unpopular conservative governments against the restive masses. However, neither military nor economic measures have been able to prevent political turmoil in some parts of Latin America. True, the alliance has succeeded, for the time being, in preventing communist takeovers, but the unpopularity of communist governments is not equivalent to sympathy for the United States. But from the American point of view, the cure has been as bad as the disease. The displacement of governments that were not viable through military *coups* has not been palatable to American tastes; at the same time, the military cliques have no marked fondness for the United States. Moreover, military dictatorships in the Western Hemisphere may ultimately stimulate the growth of communism in the Americas and blacken the United States' image in other parts of the world.

By working for social reforms while being forced to channel aid through established governments, the United States has incurred the ire of the right and the distrust of the left. It is hard to identify friends of the United States among actual or potential leading groups. The middle class is small and insignificant. The new managerial class has often been reluctant to help in instituting needed reforms. It has identified itself, largely for reasons of social status, with the interests of the feudal nobility, at whom the American reform program is aimed. For that reason, the managers carry little weight among the masses and would be ineffectual, even if they were willing, in aiding American purposes. The United States has been left little choice but to work through existing channels even if this has meant dealing with unfriendly traditional elites. Moreover, it has been unable to avoid the dilemma of being caught between supporting unpopular governments and intervention. By trying to evade the issue it has often antagonized those supporting social change as well as those resisting it.

The dilemma confronting American statesmen is the intensity of the revolutionary force behind the liberation movements in the newly rising nations. In many instances, the need and desire for political reconstruction vastly overshadows the desire for economic improvement and mod-

ernization. Such political aspirations are not easily reconciled with strategic American interests, whereas they blend
ideally with Soviet policy. The Soviet Union is interested
in penetrating uncommitted areas and easing communist
opposition. The Soviet Union has set out to undermine the
stability of regimes resisting its influence through the novelty and vigor of the communist idea, against which tired
and ineffective governments are often defenseless. The
American reaction, naturally, has consisted in efforts to
fortify vulnerable countries against communist penetration
by strengthening political stability. However, stability per
se is too vague a concept to provide a workable core of
concrete policies. To ascertain what will promote stability
in a given situation, it is necessary to analyze the particular circumstances and the effects that alternative policies
are likely to produce. It is understandable that concern
with stability should find its practical expression in a policy
aimed at the maintenance of the status quo, not only in
the international realm but, in view of the nature of cold
warfare, also in domestic politics. But it is precisely this
preoccupation that has forced the United States into its
disadvantageous defensive position. The result has often
been the opposite of what had been expected. The support
of a status quo that is not viable will more likely increase
political ferment than check it.

One could, of course, argue that the interest of the
United States as the status quo power in the bipolar world
is served well if other countries preserve their integrity in
the face of Soviet penetration, even if these countries are
immune to American influence. It should, therefore, be
possible to base thinking, for the purposes of American
foreign policy, on the easily acceptable principle of national self-determination. The problems of American foreign policy should, thereby, be much smaller than those
of the Soviets, who must exercise positive influence to attain their goal of changing the world. Unfortunately, in
practice the formula is not so simple. Commitment to self-
determination involves the United States in the often embarrassing and hazardous policy of containment. Moreover, recipients of American aid and guidance cannot

easily be convinced that they can remain impervious to American influence, and their governments are thereby often rendered vulnerable to communist attacks. In addition, communist methods and ideas do appear attractive in many instances and require more positive countermeasures than mere advocacy of independence. It should also not be overlooked that national self-determination frequently presents a direct challenge to the status quo and is likely to involve the United States in embarrassing contradictions. The principle of self-determination is difficult to propound; it relaxes discipline within the American camp and is hazardous to use against the opponent. It could be used to stir up revolts within the communist camp, but if it were effective, the United States would be confronted with the alternatives of risking general war by aiding the insurgents or losing prestige by failing to stand behind its ideology. Self-determination as a political weapon has great potential utility, but only if used discriminately. The United States has been aware of that danger and interestingly enough has enjoined its propaganda agencies not to encourage an uprising in East Germany. Great as the temptation must be to stir up ferment in the enemy camp, the Berlin uprising of 1953 and the Hungarian revolution of 1956 had taught that it is more prudent not to put the doctrine to a test.

The possibility remains that the United States might take the ideological offensive. It has taken the lead in the past decade in proclaiming lofty principles and also in aiding the liberation of the masses of Asia, Africa, and South America from political oppression and economic exploitation by colonial administrations and native elites. Such efforts have usually been accompanied by the pronouncement of ideological principles. A striking example is President Kennedy's declaration of principles in announcing the Alliance for Progress; the appeal was directed at the populist forces, reminding them of the revolutionary commitment of the United States, begun in 1776 but not yet finished. Kennedy said, "Our hemisphere's mission is not yet complete. For our unfulfilled task is to demonstrate to the entire world that man's unsatisfied aspiration for economic

progress and social justice can best be achieved by free
men working within the framework of democratic institutions." He offered American help to combat illiteracy, improve the productivity and use of land, wipe out disease,
attack archaic tax and land tenure structures, provide edu-
cational opportunities, and make the benefits of increasing
abundance available to all. "All the people of the hemisphere must be allowed to share in the expanding wonders
of modern science." And he concluded, "Let us once again
transform the American continents into a vast crucible of
revolutionary ideas and efforts . . . an example to all the
world that liberty and progress walk hand in hand." [15]

In this particular instance, the ideological attack was
part of a massive ideological, political, and economic offensive and had considerable plausibility. The purpose was
not conversion or ideological conquest of the world but
the acquisition of sturdy allies. However, Americans in
positions of influence have frequently not had a clear conception of the proper order of priority and have repeatedly
tended to place ideological ends above strategic interests.
An example of that confusion was the report of the Clay
Committee, *The Scope and Distribution of United States
Military and Economic Assistance Programs,* published in
March 1963.[16] It proposed to judge American foreign assistance programs on the basis of "the sharp criterion of
their value to the security of our country and of the free
world" without insisting "upon the establishment of our
own economic system." But the stated purpose is belied
by the substance of the report. Without considering the
effects upon foreign policy or the specific needs of particular countries, it censured aid granted for establishing "gov-
ernment-owned industrial and commercial enterprises which
compete with private endeavors" and warned against extending "aid which is inconsistent with our beliefs, democratic tradition, and knowledge of economic organization
and consequences."

A similar note was sounded in an address by former
Vice President Nixon, in which he warned against any
"aid which is to be used by the recipient nation for social-
izing or nationalizing a basic industry." Emphasizing uni-

versal political freedom, Mr. Nixon said, "I say that it is time for us proudly to declare that our ideas are for export . . ."; he concluded with an appeal "not just to defend freedom but also to extend it and share it with others throughout the world." [17] Unfortunately neither the Clay Report nor Mr. Nixon made any attempt to explain the connection between these ideological pronouncements and the security or political interests of the United States. Although Mr. Nixon at that time was not a spokesman for the United States government, his remarks merit attention because of his continuing influence in American politics.

To the political observer, such leanings toward ideological crusading raise some fundamental questions. One pertains to the implicit belief that the American ideology is or can be universally attractive. Actually, it seems doubtful that the liberal-democratic ideology is sufficiently in tune with the needs and problems of the twentieth century to promise success. The individualism on which it is based is little honored in contemporary collectivist societies, and its faith in the harmony of interests does not fit a world torn by the tensions that invariably accompany industrialism. The priority that liberalism places on individual freedom has lost much of its appeal in advanced Western societies—its original home—where concern with material well-being and luxury has come to overshadow libertarian ideals. For the rising nations of Africa and Asia, for whom social justice and national independence are the highest goals, it has no meaning. The social struggle in which they are engaged requires political action rather than debates in press and parliament as ends in their own right. Especially when overwhelming confusion and disorder have followed political emancipation, parliamentary democracy with its dissensions and divisions has evoked considerable skepticism.

The obsolescence of the democratic ideology is difficult, if not impossible, to overcome, and attempts at modernization are handicapped by the rationalistic premises of the American creed. Certainly, experience holds small hope for the supremacy of reason in human conduct and casts considerable doubt on the validity of the concomitant assumptions of the self-assertive power of truth and the self-enforceability of democracy. The American belief in the power of truth has eliminated the need for serious propaganda efforts. In issuing directives to his staff stressing the importance of objective news reporting on the basis of truth,[18] the director of the United States Information Agency, for example, has showed no evident concern for the selection of facts so as to strike the adversary where he is most vulnerable. Selection in all reporting and deliberate efforts to expose sensational and superficially plausible half-truths or untruths are not part of this ideological framework.

A similar problem exists with reference to the establishment of democracy. Not enough thought has been given to the implementation of democratic ideological appeals, since the masses, at whom such appeals are aimed, are expected to embrace spontaneously the democratic creed for its evident superiority. This expectation is especially unrealistic when the requisite preconditions do not exist. Democracy is not likely to be a feasible system when a high degree of social differentiation or a differentiated status of the sexes or generations prevails.

The improbability that the liberal-democratic ideology as propagated by the United States will win wide acceptance in underdeveloped countries does not mean that American propaganda efforts have been ineffective. If the results have not been those sought by the United States, the explanation lies chiefly in the ideological substance, and only to a lesser degree in the ineptitude of the propaganda agencies. A doctrine advocating assumption of governmental authority by the people does not create stability when the requisite political maturity is lacking. To be sure, when the people accept leadership of the established elite, no problem arises, but when the latter has lost popular support, the doctrine has revolutionary implications. It would be naive to think that revolutionary proclivities aroused in this manner are stymied by institutional democracy. There is no evidence that democracies are necessarily peaceful or that there is anything inherent in democracy compelling stability. If anything, the open and dynamic group life of democratic societies tends to promote instability and render them particularly vulnerable to communist infiltration.

Even faced with such obstacles, the ideological offensive might be salvaged if the United States could support leadership that was able and willing to lead the people in the desired direction. Unfortunately, it is difficult to make leaders receptive to American goals. In most instances, popular opinion favors those who are or have, until recently, been opposed to established regimes. The best organized opposition in backward countries is usually provided by communists. Of course, not all strong populist leaders are communists. But even noncommunist leaders are not likely to be receptive to the rationalist premises of liberal ideology or to be greatly impressed with rational refutations of Marxian fallacies. Because of domestic politics, they depend on the favor of the masses, which are anti-Western and believe that communism will satisfy their national and social cravings. To such men, a show of military strength tempered by tangible promises will often be more persuasive than the prospect of freedom and human dignity. This is the lesson implied by the Suez episode and by Soviet resumption of atmospheric nuclear tests in the early 1960's. In neither instance did American good will and sincerity wipe out Soviet gains. Chances that the United States will "out-revolutionize the world," then, are not great, and in view of the anti-American leanings of the underdeveloped peoples one may question the wisdom of relying on the promotion of democracy as a universally effective panacea.

It is apparent, then, that the United States must seize the offensive in nonmilitary areas if it wants to hold the line. This, however, as our discussion of the ideological offensive has shown, is a difficult task for a power committed to maintaining the international status quo. American foreign policy has rightly stressed the need for political stability to check communist advances. But in a rapidly changing world, stability can only be relative and is, therefore, not identical with the domestic status quo. To ensure the degree of stability needed to combat the communist threat, it will be necessary for the United States to give political direction to countries in the process of technological development. To reconcile its own end of preserving international security for its sphere with the need for development of the rising nations, the United States will have to accept the legitimacy of the latters' new collective aspirations, and this implies emancipation from its ideological fixations. It is erroneous to think that under present conditions the international status quo necessarily coincides with the domestic status quo in areas to be defended against communist takeovers. Although the predicament of American policymakers has largely resulted from the strategic position of the United States in the bipolar system, American leaders have often been guilty of avoidable errors. The disadvantages of position are not such as to justify fatalistic resignation. Despite the inherent difficulties and the more than average bungling, the American cause is far from hopeless.

One fundamental and harmful contradiction in American foreign policymaking could be easily remedied. The United States has been generally lax in developing a comprehensive political strategy and has tended to deal with each issue as it arises based on its individual merit. At the same time, decisions have often been made mechanically, following a general formula derived from simple ideological precepts or from past experiences, regardless of their applicability to the issue at hand. However plain the dichotomy between the blessing of democracy and the evil of communism may appear to men caught up in the web of bipolar thinking, it is entirely too simple a framework to provide solutions for complex international problems. To view the world in terms of such clearcut contrasts not only is naive, but has also been the source of two major diplomatic weaknesses. It has fostered a paranoid tendency to suspect communist instigation behind every populist revolution or colonial revolt. The inadequacy of such an analysis has led the United States blindly to oppose such movements instead of ascertaining the local grievances producing them and dealing with the issues on their own terms. The second weakness has been the assumption that economic policies that were successful in Europe would be equally appropriate in less developed, non-European countries. American policymakers clearly have the power to redirect their thinking along more realistic lines.

The dim prospects of American ideological offensives are no cause for despair. In spite of appearances, the sympathies that the Soviet Union has evoked in underdeveloped areas frequently do not have any ideological basis. For example, Latin America has shown little receptivity to communist principles and ideas, demonstrating that the ideological commitment is not very deep. Whatever inroads communism has made or is making are largely an expression of resentments against North American hegemony and capitalism rather than an ideological commitment. The United States has in fact taken positive steps to salvage the Alliance for Progress through support for a program of Latin American economic integration adopted at the Punta del Este conference of April 1967 by seventeen of the twenty Latin American states.[19] Although many obstacles, particularly the poorer states' fear of being swallowed up by their more powerful brethren, will have to be overcome before the plan can be implemented,[20] the Punta del Este resolution possibly marks the beginning of a new era in United States-Latin American relations. It is noteworthy that most of the states apparently reject the Cuban formula for solving their problems and, despite their growing determination to follow an independent foreign policy, are looking to a joint regional effort in cooperation with the United States. An additional new development is the evident decline on the part of the large countries of their traditional hostility to collective enterprises involving the United States; these states are among the staunchest supporters of the plan.

In reality, Soviet policy has been rather pragmatic. The Soviet Union has been cautious in its use of the ideological tack in countries that are not susceptible to communism. Whatever successes it has scored in such countries have resulted from careful exploitation of anti-Western and anti-American resentments rather than from ideology. Although the Soviet Union has the advantage of not being afflicted with colonialist liabilities, it does not enjoy universal popu-

larity in the former colonial world, and its cold war strategies have not met with exceptional success. The United
States could score significant successes against the Soviet
Union if it proceeded with equal pragmatism, concentrat-
ing on the exploitation of communist weaknesses rather
than on its own moral and ideological superiority. The
ideological weapon may sometimes be useful; but indis-
criminate preaching of the gospel of capitalist democracy
without regard to the conditions and needs of the people
involved will hardly prove an effective antidote to communist expansion. The economic needs of underdeveloped
countries are both real and urgent. To alleviate their suffering is not only a humanitarian obligation, but a strategic
necessity. However, it would be unrealistic to think that
the desire for economic improvement takes precedence
over a craving for national independence and social justice.

CHAPTER FIVE

THE SUPERPOWERS AND THEIR CLIENTELE

One of the more noteworthy aspects of the superpowers' cold war strategies is the central importance of third states. This may seem strange at first, in view of the unrivaled destructive capabilities of the Big Two. Evidently, no straight-line relationship exists between leaders and followers. Their overwhelming military strength does not enable the superpowers to manipulate their allies or the neutrals who have come to lean on them. On the contrary, relations with such friends require the utmost caution and tact, as experiences of both the United States and the Soviet Union have shown.

American leaders have candidly admitted that the United States does not desire unilateral action, and that involvements in Europe and Vietnam are matters of the greatest urgency lest the United States surrender important positions. Soviet leaders have been less inclined to such open admissions, but their competition for allies has been both obvious and vigorous. Although the competition has occasionally been relaxed, the alliance problem has occupied a central position in the policies of both superpowers. To avoid neglecting their relations with others, the superpowers were given a reminder by the Secretary-General of the

United Nations in his annual report for the year ending June 15, 1961. Speaking as a disinterested party, he emphasized the need of the big powers to be considerate of other nations. An attempt will now be made, first, to explain the value of allies to the superpowers, and second, to analyze the nature of the relationship between leaders and followers.

THE IMPORTANCE OF ALLIES

It is not difficult to suggest psychological reasons for the two superpowers wanting to forge alliance systems. Great powers have a natural tendency to enlist allies and stake out spheres of influence. It was especially natural for the United States and the Soviet Union to do so during the formative, early years of bipolarization toward the end of the Second World War, when the pattern of international power was still following territorial lines. However, as both became first-rate nuclear powers, and the radical changes in arms technology revolutionized strategic concepts, the rationale of their persisting interest in allies was no longer clear-cut. Third powers have little weight in tipping the scales of the nuclear balance, and in a nuclear confrontation the presence or absence of allies seems to be of little importance. How, then, can one account for the continued solicitude of the superpowers for alliances?

It may be conceded, perhaps, that natural inclination and traditional thinking played a part despite diminishing relevance to existing conditions. However, it seems doubtful that a policy as costly as collecting allies would have endured in the absence of practical reasons. In spite of both the economic and military liabilities that they represent and their modest military contributions to the Korean and Vietnamese campaigns, allies can strengthen the position of the nuclear powers in a number of ways. Territorial positions, manpower, and access to raw materials may be of direct value to the superpower or, at least, may appear desirable enough to keep out of the opponent's reach. True, such advantages lose much of their value in the face of nuclear warfare, where readily available, zeroed-in weapons are likely to bring instantaneous and universal destruction.

Moreover, the military value of territorial bases has been largely eliminated by the development of mobile maritime missile bases. But to focus attention exclusively on nuclear strategy is to misjudge the essence of contemporary international politics. The "unthinkability" of nuclear war has not resulted in the termination of the bipolar struggle, even though it has profoundly affected the form which the contest has assumed. It must be remembered that nuclear armaments and nuclear strategy only provide the backdrop against which the contest takes place, inasmuch as the purpose of the nuclear establishment is deterrence rather than utilization. The expectation of an actual engagement of nuclear devices, if it is entertained at all, is limited to a last resort in the event of a crisis. The actual contest, therefore, consists chiefly of political warfare, and when military action is resorted to, it has been, and may be expected to continue to be, of the non-nuclear variety.

Despite the great emphasis laid on establishing nuclear positions, the superpowers have not become indifferent to the need for drawing and maintaining a territorial line between themselves. Even in a world dominated by nuclear strategy and nuclear calculations, the opponent must be held at bay; a stand has to be taken somewhere. In this effort, allies continue to have considerable strategic importance. Their military value in deterring or, if necessary, fighting limited wars ranks high in the calculations of the superpowers. However insignificant their positive military support may be, it would be unwise, perhaps even impossible, to dispense with their contribution of bases for the superpowers' troops, raw and, especially, fissionable materials, and, most importantly, legal grounds for superpower intervention in order to secure an area against the encroachments of an opponent. The importance of allies is even greater in the political arena. Both superpowers set a high premium on voting majorities in the United Nations and at international conferences. Although allies cannot always be counted on to give such support, they are more likely to do so than are uncommitted countries. Since the political contest is largely a propaganda war, it is understandable that the leading powers should be vitally concerned with a favorable world opinion within the United Nations and elsewhere. Accordingly, they spare no effort to enlist as much support as possible.

Political and strategic reasons, then, explain the inordinate interest of the superpowers in building and maintaining alliances. Their search for security also explains the length to which they will go to prevent an ally from slipping out of their control and their incessant efforts to extend their influence to uncommitted countries and, if possible, to the opponent's defected allies. Thus, the integration of allies into comprehensive defense systems and effective guidance of their basic foreign policies becomes a major preoccupation. The defection of an ally or any loss of influence seems a cause of alarm since it can amount to a double increase in the opponent's relative strength.

To complete the appraisal, it is essential to recognize that allies can also be serious liabilities. The need to provide effective protection for them could possibly involve the leading power in a nuclear war. Europe, in particular, represents such a potential liability to the United States because of its vulnerability to Soviet attack. It is entirely possible that the United States might feel compelled to respond with massive retaliation were such an attack to occur. Moreover, an ally may conceivably become aggressive for reasons of its own. Although none of the allies could presently wage a nuclear war, some are entirely capable of starting one. To forestall such a contingency, the United States has maintained a fleet in the Taiwan Straits, whose object is not only to protect Taiwan but also to restrain Chiang Kai-shek from attacking the Chinese mainland. Similar considerations have been behind American reluctance to share nuclear weapons with its NATO allies except on American terms and under American control.

The Soviets, too, can be burdened by allies as is well illustrated by Soviet relations with Castro's Cuba. Castro has been an uncomfortable ally, who has repeatedly embarrassed the Soviet Union through his intransigence and aggressiveness. His unwillingness to permit United Nations inspection of missile installations after the American-Russian showdown in 1962 almost wrecked arrangements for a peaceful settlement. The Soviet Union has since made efforts to restrain Castro's hostility to the United States, and it is, no doubt, at Soviet instigation that he has adopted a more conciliatory tone.[1] A far more massive liability to the Soviet Union has been its relations with China. Chinese pressure has repeatedly increased cold war tensions and forced the Soviet Union to pursue more adventurous policies than it considered expedient. A further illustration is the Egyptian provocation of Israel in the spring of 1967. Although the Soviet Union has encouraged ferment in the Middle East, it seems unlikely that it anticipated or approved the degree of Arab militancy at that time. The defeat of Arab military forces confronted the Soviet Union with the unpleasant alternatives of risking a confrontation with the United States or suffering a serious political setback in world politics. Although the crusading zeal and lack of political realism on the part of the Arab states has appreciably strengthened the influence of the Soviet Union in the Middle East, it seems unlikely that the Soviet Union will press for complete integration of these clients into its alliance system because of the inherent risk of war with the United States should the Arabs decide to fight again.

In addition to being strategic liabilities, allies have also been formidable economic burdens. The returns on investments made in them have frequently been disappointing. Here, too, the Cuban situation serves as an illustration. The Soviet Union has pumped enormous sums into Cuba, which has turned out to be a bottomless pit, and has received, in return, neither appreciable advantages nor loyalty. Since the missile base fiasco in 1962, Cuba's value has been little more than as an irritant in the flank of the United States. South Vietnam has been similarly disappointing to the Americans. Continuous heavy investments have failed to build up the country to a point where it was able to repel the communist onslaught.

The most difficult problem arises from the occasional need to intervene in an ally's domestic affairs to ensure intrabloc harmony and stability. Although the desired goals can normally be attained through indirect and subtle methods, such as economic support, propaganda, or political manipulation, military intervention may become necessary, causing the intervening power serious political setbacks in world opinion. The Soviet Union experienced such embarrassment as a result of its direct and open interventions in Eastern Europe. Military action produced favorable immediate results by steadying a shaky regime in East Germany and restoring an orthodox communist government in Hungary. Threats of military intervention were employed with varying success in Czechoslovakia, Poland, and Yugoslavia. However, the long-range result was a loss of face for the Soviet Union throughout the world.

The United States has generally been more successful in avoiding direct involvements. Economic pressures have often been adequate means of control, and when they have failed, the United States has usually been in a better position than the Soviet Union to tolerate defections because of the greater liberality of its alliances. In Cuba the United States came close to intervening, but managed to avoid taking the final step. The one case in which American attempts to guide an ally have reached a deadlock has been South Vietnam. When it became apparent that in giving sizable financial and military aid to Ngo Dinh Diem, the United States was supporting an antidemocratic and oppressive government, the United States was in for a grim Hobson's choice: Withdrawal of support would ensure a communist victory; continuation of support would brand the United States as the friend of dictators and oppressors. The situation did not improve after Diem's government was overthrown through a military *coup*. The new government produced neither political stability nor an increased ability to repel the North Vietnamese. To hold the communists at bay and protect an ally, the United States was eventually forced into extensive and unrewarding belligerency in Vietnam.

Despite the burden which alliances entail, they are indispensable in the cold war. Neither of the superpowers could let itself be confined to a progressively narrow territory. The defense of the existing territorial distribution could certainly not be accomplished without the help of allies. In their absence, the ultimate answer to an expansionist opponent could only be all-out war. Alliances, then, are essential to keep the cold war cold and to limit the local wars that do occur. The desire of both superpowers to avoid a major war assures the allies of a central position in cold war strategies.

HEGEMONIAL NATURE OF ALLIANCES

The similarity of problems confronting the two superpowers makes it seem reasonable to consider the American and Soviet alliances under the common heading of "hegemonial alliances" and to stress such resemblances in structure and procedure as exist. The fact that both the United States and the Soviet Union occupy a hegemonial position among their respective allies can be shown without great difficulty. It can be further shown that it is not sinister motives but compelling strategic reasons that have led the superpowers to seek control over their allies; the pressure of bipolarism has driven them to extend their radius of control, if for no other reason than to contain the opponent, and to assert their leading position within their orbits. It must also be recalled that they both share an overwhelming desire to maintain peace, which is an additional incentive to secure control over allies. It is understandable, then, that the maintenance of a viable hegemonial system has been an important concern for both.

The contention that fundamental similarities exist is not invalidated by the evident contrast between the mutuality of relations in the American bloc and the tendency toward unilateralism characteristic of the Soviet style of bloc-leadership. The type of leadership determines the degree of control exercised, and therefore merits elaboration. The chief difference lies in the latitude that the hegemonial powers have considered compatible with their vital interests and in the means they have used to maintain or restore unity. The American system does not show the oppressive features that are repeatedly revealed by the Soviet system. The contributions that American allies are required to make to the common defense and to foreign aid programs has been less burdensome than those required of the Soviet Union's European allies. Consisting of independent governments of allied states, the Western alliance has been characterized by rather extensive pluralism. The United States has, therefore, emphasized persuasion and consultation on common problems. Its economic and technological superiority has enabled it to extend a helping hand and give direction, thus somewhat alleviating allied fear of the expansionism of the Soviet dictatorship.

In contrast, Soviet control has been more direct and, at times, more forcible. There has been far greater concern with uniformity, partly out of a pseudoreligious desire to preserve orthodoxy and partly as a result of practices emanating from Soviet historical experiences. Although military interventions have ceased to be a favorite device, pressures, direct or indirect, have been strong. In particular, the Soviet Union has taken a hand in the internal affairs of allied countries with great frequency. It has been in a better position to do this than the United States has because many of the allied governments composed of loyal communists tend to be susceptible to influences emanating from Moscow through the Communist Party apparatus, which is frequently aided by the not too distant presence of the Red Army.

Obstacles to Integration

The unique power of the Big Two and the seriousness with which they have sought control over their allies has not prevented a gradual loosening of both their hegemonial systems. The reason is not so much in the actual working of hegemonial relations; such relations are not necessarily oppressive. In fact, they frequently imply some very real material benefits for the allies, such as economic aid and relief from costly defense burdens. These latter-day hegemonies are uniquely different from their historical precursors in the virtual absence of onerous tributes. Although the allies are obliged to assume a reasonable share of the common effort, the leaders give far more than they exact from their allies. The chief difficulty has emanated from the nationalistic wave that is sweeping through the world. Although the centralization of power, made possible by contemporary technology, and the corresponding decline of the relative power of the nation-state has given nationalism an anachronistic character, it still remains a factor in foreign affairs. Indeed, it has proved a real stumbling-block to the consolidation of the two camps. Intrabloc relations have been beset by resistances and clashes of interests. The nationalistic upsurge of colonial peoples, in particular, has turned out to be more serious than one might have supposed. The liberal political values that the native peoples have absorbed from their imperial masters have made the liberalization, and frequently even the complete renunciation, of colonial imperialism a serious obligation. Especially after the encouragement they had received through the Atlantic Charter, national and racial aspirations became too powerful to be resisted or repressed. Since the end of the Second World War, colonial and semidependent peoples everywhere have risen against the white man's rule. The United States has generally lived up to its promises to support the demands of formerly dependent peoples for independence. But in doing so, it was caught up in the dilemma of seeing the newly emancipated nations drawn into the bipolar competition just as the colonial ties were severed. While pressing for emancipation, the United States had to make sure that it would have the cooperation of the new nations in international policy. Consequently, the task of American postwar foreign policy in the colonial world has been to liquidate imperialism while simultaneously integrating the newly emancipated peoples into its security system.

In Europe and Latin America, a different problem has developed. In these areas, the need for integration has meant reducing the autonomy of hitherto independent peoples by securing a controlling influence over their international and, to some extent, their domestic affairs while avoiding any overt manifestations of external control.

Since the intensity of nationalistic feelings has precluded the direct and formal domination of allies, the superpowers have endeavored to attain their goals by drawing their friends into partnerships under their aegis. In this way, the two leading powers have achieved a practical compromise between national diversity and central control. Nevertheless, it remains an open question as to how satisfactory this arrangement has been. Evidently, hegemonial control within the context of an alliance is rarely complete, and its limits are often difficult to estimate. The characteristic reciprocity of allied relations normally results in a precarious balance that may variously incline toward either decentralization or hegemonial control. The only generalization that can be confidently made is that the liberality of the formal structure alone is no proof of the de facto independence of the lesser sovereignties. That the United States has proclaimed the extension of freedom as the chief objective of its foreign policy is not necessarily an indication of altruistic motivations. In terms of power, freedom, in the classical liberal sense, means the minimization of Soviet influence and the maintenance of open channels for American influence.

Despite the resurgence of nationalism, the first years after the Second World War witnessed rather tight hegemonial relations, rarely marred by any significant resistance of allies to superpower control. The Soviet orbit, in particular, was quite properly described as a system of satellites. Its approximation of a communist monolith seemed to vindicate the Marxian expectation of world communist unity. At that time, the American camp also presented a fairly united front, and the United States succeeded, to a high degree, in wielding a controlling influence over its allies. The reasons for the submissiveness of the allies are not difficult to find. The political and economic life of the European countries, which now found themselves in one camp or the other, had been seriously disrupted during the war, and their need to lean upon a strong power was great. Their dependence on the Big Two was further increased by the enormous military prestige the latter had gained in defeating Germany. The tendency to look to the Big Two for guidance was also strengthened by the ideological character of the struggle against Nazi Germany and the desire to identify either with the great liberal power in the West or the great communist power in the East. Both seemed to represent the democratic aspirations of the world, although in different forms.

The docility of the allies, however, did not endure. Their apathy subsided as their countries recovered from the ravages of war. Before a decade had elapsed, they had regained their national consciousness and were ready to assert their independence. The one-time approximation of the communist monolith broke up, and it was no longer possible to speak of a world communist movement. Directions from the communist center in Moscow, if they are attempted, could no longer be counted upon to evoke universal compliance. Therefore, the Soviet Union had no choice but to substitute a complex pattern of hegemonial relations for the former straight-line relationship. After taking account of the growing nationalism, sharp conflicts of interest, and pressures for a higher standard of living and increased personal freedom, which have been especially evident in Eastern Europe since Stalin's death, the Soviet Union relaxed its direct control. Instead, its predominance in the region rests on economic and organizational ties, enmeshing the various countries in an intricate pattern of economic, military, and cultural relations, and making it impossible for any of them to withdraw without risking serious social disruption. Threats of military action and interventions, effective means of control in the late 1940's and the 1950's, seem highly impractical today.

In the case of the American bloc, with its more relaxed hegemonial relations, the self-assertion of the allies has been a less radical change, but it has been a change nonetheless. Even the generous American aid programs, which should have gone far to assuage animosities, have not always been well received. In Europe, American generosity has evoked distrust and envy; in the underdeveloped countries it has given rise to the suspicion that imperialism was returning in a new guise. Here, as in the Soviet camp, the difficulties arising from the nationalistic upsurge have been aggravated by objective problems, such as the frequent lack of unity of purpose between the superpowers and their allies, or disagreements between the allies themselves, which in some instances seem too fundamental to be reconcilable.

On the American side, the allied problem stands out most clearly in the relations with the European allies, who have been anxious to disengage themselves from their close link to the United States despite ideological affinities and the shared determination to stem communist expansion. In fact, as a result of American help, the European nations became economically and militarily more independent, and this gave new impetus to the separatist tendencies. France, in particular, has insisted on pursuing policies of its own, with little regard for their compatibility with American aims. It has begun to develop a national nuclear force, vetoed British membership in the Common Market, made an independent bid for Soviet friendship, sought trade with Cuba, and recognized Communist China. The high point of French independence was reached in 1966 with the withdrawal of French forces from the integrated allied defense organization and with the request that all United States and Canadian military bases in France be liquidated and the Supreme Headquarters of NATO be removed from French soil.

The self-assertions of European nations are more clearly based on sentimentalities than on a realistic appraisal of their military capabilities. Many have found the decline of their power and position hard to accept; they look nostalgically to past glories. De Gaulle certainly entertains the ambition of recapturing France's leading position in world politics. In this endeavor, he has challenged American leadership not only in Europe but in Africa, Asia, and Latin America. European nationalism has received further impetus from the democratic temper of the times. Governments have been prone to resist external control and influence when the temper of their peoples has made resistance appear politically propitious. Statesmen may be able to settle differences in private conferences, but in addressing their peoples they may find an angry nationalistic tone more profitable. It is little wonder that the fusion of nationalism and democracy should have rendered the NATO nations highly sensitive to anything resembling a loss of independence, or that the nations strove to attain a greater measure of de facto independence through such cooperative arrangements as the Common Market.

To call attention to the disparity between aspirations and reality is not, to be sure, to deny all rationality to rejections of hegemonial influence. Suspicion of American designs and skepticism toward American diplomatic dexterity have inspired an awesome fear of the consequences that may result from too close an alignment with the United States. The European nations are clearly fearful of being drawn into a war in which Europe would be the battlefield. A stiffening of resistance can therefore be observed whenever the United States follows a hard line vis-à-vis the Soviet Union. Such fears are not wholly without foundation and, in view of Europe's central geographic location, are not easy to allay. For example, there was reason to fear that during the Korean War the United States might unilaterally decide to employ nuclear devices against China, with unpredictable consequences for itself and its allies. Fears were also aroused by the American blockade of Cuba, which was undertaken without previous consultation. In both cases, the allies felt themselves dangerously close to a nuclear war that they had neither provoked nor wanted.

Paradoxically, some of the European allies have been just as nervous over any relaxation of Soviet-American tensions for fear that any compromises that might be made would be at their expense. Such apprehensions are understandable. American aversion to "entangling alliances" is well remembered, and events of the postwar period have done little to remove the continental image of "Anglo-Saxon unreliability." The anti-British and anti-French stand of the United States at Suez has left deep wounds. Even more disturbing was a statement made in 1959 by Under Secretary of State Herter that he did not expect the President to involve the United States in an all-out nuclear war unless its own territory was in danger of devastation.[2] The firmness of American commitment has been further weakened by the warning of the Senate Foreign Relations Committee report on the Foreign Aid Bill in July 1966 that countries which are recipients of military assistance "should in no way interpret United States generosity as a promise to help with military forces in time of trouble." [3]

These schizophrenic tendencies of American foreign policy have been responsible for much anxiety among the European allies and have contributed a major share to NATO disharmony. There can, of course, be little doubt that the United States is committed in principle to defend Europe, where it has sounded a clear and unequivocal "hands off" warning to the Russians. What is less clear is where the line of defense will be drawn. How far will the United States let an aggressor proceed before striking? What concessions will it make to the opponent at the expense of its European allies? Such fears and uncertainties were at the bottom of Adenauer's constant warnings against a more conciliatory American attitude toward the Soviet Union and nurtured de Gaulle's desire to have a nuclear force of his own.

The difficulties that stand in the way of integrating allies have been even more marked in Southeast Asia and the Middle East. SEATO, the Southeast Asian alliance, has not had enough cohesion to be of much value. Its major shortcoming has been the absence of a community of interests among its members and among those whose territorial integrity it purports to protect. The area it is concerned with lacks the attributes of a region in the political sense. Although incipient regionalism can be detected, the sense of community is still too rudimentary to form the basis of an effective defense organization. In addition to this inherent infirmity, American purposes are being frustrated by recent memories of colonialism. The peoples of the area tend to view the Western powers with considerably greater skepticism than the powers of the East, which are not burdened with similar historical liabilities. American protection and economic aid are frequently suspected of being means to prevent the area from becoming self-sufficient, to make it increasingly dependent on Western markets and imports, and to involve it in the bipolar conflict. Even where the anticommunist purpose is firm, as in the Philippines, Thailand, and Pakistan, the alliance has shown little promise. It is not easy to convince these nations of American ability or commitment to defend them against communist attacks. The favorite weapons of aggressive communist forces are economic and political penetration and these are hard to combat. There is reason to doubt that the United States can be successful in a limited war of the guerrilla type. Consequently, the defense of the area may be assumed to rest ultimately on massive retaliation. The promise that, if necessary, the United States is willing to incur the risk of such action is more than the credulity of the allies will bear.

The Middle Eastern alliance, CENTO, is not technically an American alliance since the United States is not a member. However, it is mentioned in this context since the United States was instrumental in forming it and has pledged its cooperation in mutual defense. The United States has left no doubt as to its vital interest in preventing the members' absorption into the Soviet camp. But this system, similar to SEATO, suffers from a lack of wide membership, unity of purpose, and a profound distrust of what may appear as a return of Western colonialism.

Belatedly, Latin America has been drawn into the bipolar contest. Surprisingly, it is here that the United States has encountered some of its thorniest problems. Neither the traditional ties between the United States and its neighbors to the south, as formulated in the Monroe Doctrine, nor the Organization of American States and the defense treaty of Rio de Janeiro have been able to ensure American solidarity in the face of nonmilitary communist attempts to gain a foothold in the Western Hemisphere. Latin America, by and large, has shown little inclination to cooperate in the defense against communist ideological penetration and the occasional establishment of communist governments in the hemisphere. The communist threat has not seemed of sufficient immediacy to overcome the hypersensitivity of the southern continent to United States interference. Therefore, the organization has invariably been reluctant to sanction collective measures directed at the internal affairs of an American state in cases of communist takeovers, and even more so in the event of military *coups*. In the case of Cuba, the action of the OAS did not go beyond moral censure and a break of diplomatic relations. Cuba's political and economic isolation was not, of course, of any consequence, as long as it could trade with the rest of the world and obtain economic aid from the communist bloc.

The United States might, of course, have intervened militarily. But such action would have branded it as an imperialist power in the eyes of the world, an impression it has been anxious to avoid. For that reason it has also been treading cautiously in Panama, which has demanded renegotiation of the treaty of 1903 defining the relationship between the two countries. The American reaction to such demands has been conciliatory. How far the United States will go in meeting Panamanian demands is difficult to anticipate. Reasons of status and prestige carry much weight in political warfare. A surrender of position at Panama may set an embarrassing precedent in relation to other bases, such as Guantanamo.

For all the differences that divide Soviet-communist politics from Western-democratic politics, and that set off Soviet hegemonial leadership from American hegemonial leadership, the Soviet camp has not been immune to the disruptive effect of nationalism. Ideological uniformity has failed to produce the harmony that Marxian teachings had so confidently predicted. The Marxian doctrine of the natural and necessary solidarity of the world proletariat has not signaled the end of national divisions. The lines of control have been particularly confused by the new sovereignties, which have refused to accept the simple ideological alignment. The most spectacular display of dissension within the communist camp has been the rift between the Soviet Union and its Chinese ally. Although the clash has been largely couched in ideological terms, there is good reason to doubt that the exegesis of communist scripture is the real basis of the controversy. The animosities can be explained easily enough on other than Marxian grounds. It is natural in any circumstance that rivalry should develop between two great powers within one orbit and that the lesser of the two should feel the need for self-assertion in the face of attempts by the other to dictate policy. From

the point of view of power, China is not, at present, in
the same class as the Soviet Union despite its evident and
alleged advances in the nuclear and missile areas, but its
influence in Asia and the explosion of a hydrogen bomb
in June 1967 have been the cause of much anxiety to the
Soviets.

The conflict has been aggravated by a number of other
factors. A lack of a sense of moral indebtedness on the
part of the junior power no doubt is one. The Soviet Union
had done little to encourage the Chinese communist revolution and, when it broke out, only reluctantly supported
it. Stalin's apparent lack of concern for the welfare of the
Chinese communists not only was resented but cast doubts
on the doctrine of proletarian solidarity. Dissension has
been compounded by geographic and racial considerations.
China has increasingly come to view itself as the leading
power in Asia and has felt reassured in its aspirations by
the sympathies it has evoked among a number of Asian
communist parties. It has not been possible for the Soviet
Union to challenge the Chinese on ideological grounds.
The Chinese have insisted that the Soviet refusal to equip
China with nuclear arms is hard to reconcile with the professed solidarity of world communism. At the bottom of
the discord lie suspicions and resentments resulting from
the uneven stages of development of Soviet and Chinese
communism. The older revolutionary power, having ma-
tured sufficiently to accept and adapt itself to the world's
imperfections, has become suspect in the eyes of the
younger one, whose perfectionist zeal remains undiminished. China, therefore, frowns upon arrangements that it
considers accommodation with the enemy; the nuclear test
ban treaty, which is particularly suspect, is seen as an attempt to prevent Chinese nuclear development. Moreover
China has repeatedly accused the Soviet Union of having
entered into what amounts to an anti-Chinese alliance with
the United States. The tensions have long passed the point
of being a family secret and have barely stopped short of
an open diplomatic break. At the National Day parade in
Peking in October 1966, Soviet diplomats, followed by the
diplomats of many Soviet bloc countries, walked off the

reviewing stand in protest against charges of plotting with Washington about Vietnam.[4]

Soviet relations with the Eastern European allies have also been clouded by many outbreaks of disharmony. Open resistance occurred in East Germany, Hungary, and Poland. Albania has joined the Chinese camp; Yugoslavia has pursued an independent course; and Rumania has, for some time, consistently followed a line of resistance.

Stability of Alliances

The flexibility of hegemonial systems permits considerable variation, and power relations are never quite the same at different times. Hegemonial relations, as has been seen, have become progressively variegated with the relaxation of cold war tensions. The superpowers' assumption in the early years of the cold war that allies could be made to do their bidding through simple fiat has given way to a readiness to make concessions, and the pattern of allied relations has become extraordinarily complex. Nevertheless, the two blocs have shown remarkable stability. No ally of the United States, save Cuba and perhaps Iraq, has thus far deliberately defected, and no communist country has sided with the United States against the Soviet Union. Even France has remained in NATO after withdrawing from the integrated defense system. The close ties that continue to exist between the Soviet Union and its Eastern European allies can be clearly seen in the latter's reaction to the ouster of Khrushchev. The fear that there might again be a tightening of Soviet control after the breathing spell of the Khrushchevian era produced considerable tension. Yet the ouster did not turn into an occasion for defections, and nothing happened to suggest that the Soviet bloc was crumbling. Although the ideological discipline imposed by Moscow has not been able to prevent profound divisions within the communist world, the schism has not caused communist countries to flock to the Western camp for support. In spite of the sympathy and aid extended by the United States, Yugoslavia has remained close to the Eastern camp and has come closer to realigning itself, even if on its own terms. Nor is it likely that Rumania will radically depart from the Eastern European camp, despite its increasing assertion of independence. It is interesting to note that France apparently did not interpret an attempted rapprochement by Rumania as an indication of a serious rift with the Soviets.[5] In fact, despite all the noise of the Sino-Soviet quarrel, China has not formally severed its ties with the Soviet camp, and in such major international crises as Vietnam and the Middle East the two leading communist powers, though competitors, are on the same side.

The amount of control exercised by the hegemonial powers poses a more difficult question. The rise of formal polycentrism, the commitment of the superpowers to the liquidation of imperialism, and the actual dissolution of colonial empires do not shed much light on the matter. These are surface phenomena that do not tell us much about substantive power relations. In fact, hegemonial purposes are frequently more effectively realized through subtle devices, such as the coordination of lesser sovereignties in political alliances. In the cases of the United States and the Soviet Union, we have seen many displays of disunity within the alliances and of outright defiance of the leading powers by their allies. Moreover, allies are often effective restraining influences. To accommodate its allies, the United States refrained from invading Cuba after the communist takeover, from employing atomic weapons in the Korean War, and from recognizing East Germany when West Germany objected. Similarly, the Chinese, Yugoslav, and Rumanian sensibilities have left their imprint on Soviet foreign policy. It has been shown that allies repeatedly act independently and in defiance of the basic policies of the hegemonial powers.

Making full allowance for the latitude enjoyed by the allies, the question must be raised whether they have, in fact, succeeded in casting out the influence of the leading powers. The case of NATO, in which American designs have repeatedly been frustrated, provides a valuable source of information. The American project of transforming the defensive alliance into a genuine political, economic, and cultural community under the aegis of the United States was never successfully begun. In the course of time, the internal disunity of NATO has been on open display; the members' votes in the United Nations have been divided even on important issues. The United States could do little about France's defiance of its hegemony. The numerous concessions that had been made[6] did not prevent a French rapprochement with communist countries and open French support of the latter's policies on such important matters as the war in Vietnam, the reunification of Germany, or the flareup in the Middle East; nor have they prevented French withdrawal from the integrated defense system. However, the United States did thwart de Gaulle's efforts to break up the alliance and permanently remove the American presence from Europe.

What has made de Gaulle's moves especially threatening is the fact that his desire to liquidate the American hegemony in Europe has been shared by sizable minorities outside France. To undercut their arguments against the American presence, it was necessary to reduce unilateralism and to make relations more reciprocal. Through his "Declaration of Interdependence" on July 4, 1962, President Kennedy tried to put the European alliance on a partnership basis, assuring the allies of a voice in making decisions and the right to be informed of the strategic decisions of the United States. To make the partnership concept credible, it was necessary to back up the declaration with concrete concessions. For that reason, the United States developed a plan for a multilateral nuclear force within the context of NATO in which it would share equally with its allies veto power over employment of the force. In this way, it was hoped that the allies' nationalist aspirations could be satisfied and the fears arising from their military exposure assuaged. The most important aspect of this plan was that the collective force would have met growing pressures for nuclear sharing without nuclear proliferation and thus would have gone a long way toward meeting de Gaulle's challenge.

The involvement of the allies in making basic strategies, while affecting their relations with the leading power, does not necessarily signify the evaporation of the hegemonial authority. The project for a multilateral nuclear force failed to materialize not because the United States was going back on earlier promises but because of the reaction evoked by Germany's participation throughout Europe and in the Soviet Union. But the plan in no way implied a de facto abdication of the controlling position of the United States. Nuclear warheads stationed in Europe are under American control now and would, in effect, have remained so had they been placed at the disposal of a collective NATO force. The Supreme Commander of the NATO forces has invariably been an American general, and the great superiority of the United States in military and economic spheres makes it appear unlikely that anyone but an American will hold that position in the foreseeable future. Nor would the equal veto power have changed the situation. The fact that the United States could not have employed the collective nuclear force over the veto of an ally was of little consequence since the NATO force would not have compared in size with the nuclear force that the United States possesses in its own right. If the United States wanted to make nuclear war, it could easily do so without access to the collective force, a possibility that is open to none of the allies. Therefore, there is more than a shred of truth in de Gaulle's objection that the presumed partnership was a means of perpetuating the American hegemony over Europe. The project for nuclear sharing was, evidently, more a political device to integrate the allies and placate their nationalist sensibilities than a useful and needed strategic measure. It is also important that the offer of partnership was not repeated or reaffirmed by President Johnson.

Relations with Latin America are of a similar type. There has been much animosity and turbulence in the past. The improvement of relations in more recent times indicates that to some extent the atmosphere has been cleared. However, sufficiently strong residues of suspicion and distrust remain to preclude full cooperation. American policies relating to Latin America have often been frustrated. The Organization of American States, for example, refused to take effective action against Castro's Cuba, and Mexico and Chile have torpedoed the plan for a Western Hemisphere peace force.[7] In addition, the United States has been embarrassed by the collective diplomatic squeezes applied by Latin members of the organization.[8] However, the more important countries look to long-range cooperation with the United States and there seems no reason to doubt that in the event of a showdown they will side with the West. After earlier frustrations, the United States scored a success of some importance when it received unanimous support in the Cuban missile crisis and when, in July 1965, the members voted to impose sanctions, however imperfect, upon Cuba to block attempts to stir up a communist revolution in Venezuela. In some instances, it is quite apparent that cooperation transcends perfunctory gestures. Reportedly, Chile is considering ties with the Atlantic Alliance.[9] Argentina and Brazil too have generally been in consonance with the broad American purposes in international politics.[10] Although relations with Argentina were strained by the coup in the summer of 1966, it seems doubtful that the previous pattern will be fundamentally changed.

The Soviet Union also has been able to hold its bloc together quite well and to secure its leading influence. The organizational pattern of the Warsaw Pact, not unlike NATO, betrays definite hegemonial features. The supreme commander is a Soviet marshal and, despite many manifestations of polycentric tendencies, a reasonably well-organized and coordinated military apparatus has been developed. Although the members have been restive, there seems to be no strong pressure for breaking up the alliance. Apparently the chief objective is the emancipation of the organization from Soviet control. This seems to be Rumania's goal; it does not appear to entertain any serious hope of destroying the pact. At no time has it threatened to withdraw and in the summer of 1967 it even rejoined the organization's military exercises and reaffirmed its membership.[11] If Rumania succeeds in loosening its political ties, there remain questions concerning the degree of its independence, whether its defiance signals the end of Soviet hegemonial influence in the larger area, and whether it will bring a fundamental change in the organizational structure, rendering the hegemony ineffectual in the pursuit of Soviet foreign policy. It is too early to evaluate the meaning and effect of Rumania's withdrawal from the Budapest Conference in March 1968.

China's efforts to break up the Soviet camp or to displace the Soviet Union from its leading position have not succeeded. China has not been able to arouse widespread sympathies for its militancy against the moderate coexistence policy of the Soviet Union, which reflects more accurately the neutralist preferences of the world. In fact, it seems that China has already transcended the bounds of prudence. It has lost whatever influence it once had upon Soviet policy. Its position in the councils of world communism is also showing signs of weakening. In noncommunist countries where China influences the communist movement, it is in continuous competition with pro-Moscow and independent communist wings. In Indonesia, which despite its official neutralism had been leaning heavily toward China, communism has lost its influence, and the country has dissociated itself from the communist camp. Among communist countries that are not ready to oppose China, only Albania gives China substantial support. As for the rest of Eastern Europe, Yugoslavia has never been sympathetic to China, and an attempted rapprochement between China and Rumania has not been successful. In Asia, North Korea's insistence on a position of independence vis-à-vis both the Soviet Union and China has repudiated the latter while continuing to depend on the former.[12] The internal confusion and turbulence in China has even driven North Vietnam into the Soviet camp.[13] The Soviet Union has taken advantage of the internal turmoil in China and has waged a successful political offensive that has brought many national communist parties to its side.

The self-assertion of the allies evidently has been a source of frustration to the superpowers. The control they are able to exercise does not measure up to their desires, and it certainly has declined sharply compared with the years immediately following the Second World War. But the crucial question is not the degree of control or influence exercised in particular instances and with respect to secondary policies that may bring the superpower into conflict with an ally's particularistic interests. The relevant test is whether the alliances have sufficiently held together to enable the superpowers to protect their vital interests and to pursue their overall policies effectively. These vital interests, for the protection of which the alliances were formed, consist fundamentally in the preservation of the bipolar territorial and political pattern. The attainment of that objective has been the special responsibility of the superpowers. Moreover, during crises they have usually acted unilaterally, formulating and executing their policies without consultation with the allies. The allies may have been more or less enthusiastic in supporting such policies, but they have not been able to do much about them. Moreover, the possible consequences of the superpowers' actions would seriously affect their own welfare and, if there were to be a showdown, involve most of them, leaving them no choice but to stand by their alliance. The superpowers have spared no effort to prevent such changes in their allies' political and military alignments as would seriously disturb the present distribution of power. By and large, they have succeeded in subordinating the particularistic interests of the allies to this broad goal. Inasmuch as most of the allies themselves have an interest in preserving the present pattern, the Soviet Union can depend on the support of its allies against the United States just as the United States can depend on its allies for anti-Soviet support.

Forces of Cohesion

What, then, accounts for this stability? The persuasive influence of the superpowers is not great enough to explain their ability to maintain or rebuild their hegemonial positions. Their success, no doubt, can be explained in part by the nuclear stalemate. In contrast to the early years of the cold war, defecting allies can no longer count on a warm welcome in the opposing alliance. Neither the United States nor the Soviet Union seems much inclined at present to encourage complications that may enhance the danger of nuclear war. This is not to say that the superpowers are

meticulously refraining from interfering in the adversary'
orbit. Advantages continue to be pressed whenever this ca
be done without straining relations to the breaking poin
For example, the Soviet Union has embraced Cuba as a
ally, but it has put a damper on Cuba's aggressivenes
toward the United States. The Soviet Union has also in
stigated the proposal of the Warsaw Pact nations to th
Western European nations to abolish NATO, to liquidat
foreign bases in Europe, and to designate denuclearize
zones. Such measures, if they were adopted, would resul
in the exclusion of the United States from Europe.[14] Th
United States, in turn, has contributed to a stiffening o
Rumania's resistance against Soviet domination through i
economic policies. But these efforts are limited. The Unite
States has not actively aided separatist tendencies in th
Soviet camp. Surely, it would find it difficult to justify th
support of one communist dictator against another. More
over, if there is a question about the United States' com
mitment to the defense of NATO, what would be the pros
pect of an effective American contribution to the defens
of Yugoslavia or any other Eastern European country tha
may want to defect from the Soviet bloc?

But when all this has been acknowledged, it might sti
be argued that the nuclear stalemate provides no unequiv
ocal discouragement of fluidity; on the contrary, it i
some ways encourages it. Since the unlikelihood of an
significant military action has forced the contest into th
political arena, with the main focus on the realignment o
allies and on the attachment of uncommitted states, th
reception of the opponent's defected allies remains a stron
temptation even at the risk of new complications. Would-b
defectors, therefore, might speculate, with some reason
that their insistent solicitations may break down the re
luctance of those whose friendship they are seeking. It i
necessary, then, to give closer attention to the reasons tha
defiant allies have been unable to break up the alliance
and form independent blocs.

In probing below the surface of the existing disunity
it is possible to detect more interests to unite than to d
vide members of the respective blocs. The diminishin

crimony of the cold war has not eradicated the fear that the reasonableness of the moment may again give way to a belligerent atmosphere. Instances when a period of relaxation was brought to an abrupt end by a sudden crisis have been too frequent to assuage fears of a possible enemy attack. Such possibilities seem all the more threatening as long as conflicts touching upon the essential interests of the superpowers remain unresolved. The persistent nuclear threat understandably provides a common ground for allied unity. It should, therefore, be no surprise to find increased cohesion in both camps in periods of acute danger. During Soviet offensives against the allied presence in Berlin and during the Cuban missile crisis, the European allies rallied around American leadership, whereas peaceful gestures by the Soviet Union have invariably tended to relax discipline in the West. Similarly, consolidation occurred in Eastern Europe while the NATO multilateral force plan was being considered.

Common interest is further enhanced by ideological similarities between the hegemonial powers and most of their allies. True, the strong emphasis that has generally been laid on ideological affinity as a basic issue may find little support when the political facts are analyzed; the role of ideology in the bipolar contest is not as clear-cut as one may think. The concern at this point is the strategic value of ideology in strengthening the bond of common interest between allies. Both sides have evidently considered ideological affinity and constitutional similarity important assets. The United States has generally preferred to deal with allies having democratic-constitutional regimes and has supported, when possible, democratic forces. The Soviet Union has consolidated its control over Eastern Europe since the end of the Second World War by returning Moscow-trained communist leaders to their native lands and helping them attain leading political positions. By so extending the communist political apparatus, the Soviet Union has acquired virtual control over strategic areas. Even if the presence of like-minded governments is no guarantee of harmonious hegemonial relations, it does tend to bar defection to the enemy side, perhaps less out of loyalty than for reasons of self-preservation. For that reason the problem of de Gaulle, however irritating, is not as serious as it appears. The common Western heritage is too strong to permit either France or any other European country that has not been conquered by communism to go over to the communist side. De Gaulle would have no place to go if he were to withdraw from the Western alliance. Although he has gone far to isolate himself from the allies, he has not withdrawn from the alliance. In fact, he has made it explicit that France's withdrawal from the integrated defense system was in no way intended as a renunciation of its membership.[15]

Another point to be considered in connection with hegemonial cohesion is that hegemonial systems normally are protectorates, and the present alliances are no exception. Ideological leadership would certainly have little practical effect unless the hegemonial powers were prepared to extend effective protection to those willing to accept that leadership. The security that the protected crave applies to enemy attacks on the international as well as on the domestic level and therefore implies not only military but economic and political aid. The importance of the protective function is well illustrated by NATO. The alliance was formed in response to Soviet expansionism, which could be stemmed only through collective efforts backed by American power. Its early years coincided with the United States atomic monopoly. The stability of the alliance suffered appreciably when that monopoly was broken by Soviet atomic development and was further weakened by the increasing vulnerability of the United States to Soviet nuclear power. When the United States withdrew its protection during the Suez episode, the alliance was in disarray and was restored only after the determined stand of the United States in the Berlin and Cuban crises. A plausible case can be made that de Gaulle has pushed France's isolation from the allies as far as he did because, in his estimation, the need for protection has greatly diminished. He seems convinced that the center of the bipolar contest has moved to Asia, removing any acute threat from Europe.[16]

The role of protection can also be observed in other

areas. Whatever leadership the United States possesses in SEATO is directly attributable to its allies' need for defense against communist expansion and its readiness to assume responsibility for their protection. Conversely, the difficulties of the alliance, which have been mentioned before, have been further aggravated by doubts concerning the ability of the United States to live up to the obligations of a protector. American reluctance to provide effective aid to Laos was not reassuring. But even when the United States has given military support, as in South Vietnam, the result has been disillusioning. The Vietnamese War has been anything but an impressive display of strength; rather, it has shown that American support may mean a drawn-out war, inflicting much suffering on the allied people.

The Middle Eastern alliance system, CENTO, also illustrates this point. It is true that the alliance was stillborn: The Arabs showed little inclination to join, and Britain and Turkey relied on other alliances. However, the position of Pakistan points up a basic dilemma. Pakistan joined both SEATO and CENTO for purposes of protection. It was less concerned with the communist threat than with the Indian threat. In joining the two alliances, it hoped to secure American protection against what it regarded as Hindu imperialism. But when the United States furnished aid to India in its border war with China, Pakistan began to disengage itself from the Western alliances, which it felt could not be depended on to provide the protection it was craving. The result has been a close Pakistani rapprochement with China. At the same time, the United States has endeavored to strengthen its position in both the Middle East and Far East by stressing the importance of protection. In the spring of 1966, Secretary of State Dean Rusk reminded the CENTO assembly of the persistence of the communist threat.[17] In the summer of the same year, during a visit in Japan, he reassured the Asian allies of American nuclear protection on the periphery of China.[18]

The desire for protection has also played its part in the Soviet camp. The Warsaw Pact, the military organization of Eastern Europe, was a clear response to the formation of NATO. It owes its origin and endurance to the need for defense against a Western Europe united under the aegis of the United States. Hegemonial discipline has varied, as it has in the American alliances, with the immediacy of the threat of an enemy attack. The loosening of the system has coincided with the decrease of tension between the superpowers and the moderation of the coexistence policy followed by the Soviet Union since the reign of Khrushchev. To strengthen discipline the Soviet Union has found it useful, at times, to increase international tensions and to conjure up the specter of an international threat. The recurrent Berlin crises have often arisen for no apparent reason other than the exigencies of alliance policy. The Soviet Union has also shown growing hostility toward the United States over the war in Vietnam, and the tone of its diplomacy has shown a belligerency that has not been displayed for many years. Evidently, the failure to give convincing support to the North Vietnamese cause would take too heavy a political toll to be justifiable.

The role of protection as a means of control stands out in the Middle East crisis of 1967. To be sure, the inability of the Soviet Union to extend military protection to the Arab states in order to avoid a confrontation with the United States produced bitterness among the Arabs and loss of prestige in the world. The Soviet Union tried to compensate for the lack of military support by recouping, through political action in the United Nations General Assembly, the losses suffered by the Arab states. Although these attempts were unsuccessful, the Soviet Union scored significant gains. Its failure was not and could not be interpreted as military weakness or lack of influence. Through sustained diplomatic pressure in favor of the Arab states, within and without the United Nations, and by replacing at no cost the military equipment destroyed or lost in the war, the Soviet Union has actually strengthened its position in the Middle East. Since most of the Arab states severed relations with the United States in order to save face, they made themselves exclusively dependent on Soviet support, enabling the Soviet Union to exact a price in terms of guidance and supervision of their military policy. A change in the relations between the states accepting such support, and the Soviet Union, and probably also with native communists, can therefore be expected. It is unlikely that Egypt, the leading Arab state, will continue to enjoy the former independence from Soviet influence and from domestic communist pressures. The Soviet Union has, in effect, made considerable progress in attaining political control over the Middle East since the Arabs are appreciably more susceptible to big power influence in defeat than they would have been in victory. Their increased need for protection has produced a tractability that ideological attacks and military aid failed to attain before their defeat.

The bearing of protective power upon the cohesion of the alliances can be understood most clearly by examining the failure of China and France to break up the hegemonial blocs. The relevant test of their success is not found in the rousing ovations that Mao Tse-tung and de Gaulle have received in Africa, Asia, and Latin America. The real test is their failure to obtain any sustained political following. Whatever the grievances of allied or uncommitted countries against the leading powers, they are not willing to forego the unique benefits derived from these associations. Neither France nor China can create the expectation in the world that its success in detonating nuclear devices and its preparations to enter the space race will elevate it to the status of a nuclear power in the near future. Being a nuclear power of comparable standing to the United States and the Soviet Union clearly requires more than a stockpile of bombs and missiles. Nuclear deterrence is not static, but, if it is to be effective, requires continuous research and development in the absence of which the nuclear arsenal quickly becomes obsolete. Both the United States and the Soviet Union have spent billions of dollars on nuclear and missile developments in order to maintain an effective, modern force. At present, no other country can afford expenditures of such staggering proportions. The efforts made by Great Britain and France in the direction of nuclear development have not been able to prevent the gap from widening between American nuclear capabilities and their own. In fact, the current trend seems to indicate the opposite. Many countries wish to be relieved of the burden of nuclear defense and prefer to rely on the protection the United States can provide. It is noteworthy that even an eminent power like Great Britain has asked for American help in reducing its defense cost.[19] Few countries seem to harbor any illusions that, for the time being, long-range protection can come from anywhere but Washington or Moscow.

Such obvious considerations have been sufficient to prevent the rise of independent blocs. The European allies, clearly, have preferred the military power of the United States to de Gaulle's rhetoric. The hegemonial position of the United States has been further strengthened by disunity among its allies. Disharmony, generally a source of embarrassment to hegemonial powers, has not only caused the allies to turn their back on de Gaulle's independent nuclear force, but has given rise to serious misgivings regarding the American plan for nuclear sharing. Aside from the cost and the problems entailed in the possession of a nuclear force, they evidently distrust each other more than they distrust the United States; in particular, they have been reluctant to give Germany a "finger on the nuclear trigger." This is not as surprising an attitude as may appear at first sight. To an extent, hegemonial position tends to be self-perpetuating in that the hegemonial power, removed from local squabbles, is often looked upon as an arbiter among the allies. De Gaulle's schismatic maneuvers, therefore, may not have any serious implications. His independent policy has reduced rather than strengthened French influence in world politics. By isolating himself from the Western bloc, he has put the world on notice that he can neither speak for the United States nor exert any influence. His anti-American stand in relation to Vietnam has produced no noticeable effects; it has failed to promote a settlement or to induce the United States' withdrawal. His *volte face* concerning Israel has neither hurt the United States nor helped the Soviet Union win a victory in the United Nations. His support of French nationalism in Canada in the summer of 1967 is unlikely to

precipitate secession, and his subsequent exhortation that
Poland loosen its ties to the Soviet Union was soundly
rebuffed by the Polish government.

An independent French policy cannot prevent war, and
as long as the United States stands by its commitment to
defend Western Europe, de Gaulle cannot secede. For that
reason, his negotiations with Moscow have had no significant tangible results. Moscow, more than anyone else,
knows that serious negotiations are possible only with the
United States.[20] There is no reason to believe that de
Gaulle was harboring great illusions or that he expected to
conclude any political agreements during his visit in June
1966.[21] He has repeatedly professed his loyalty to the Western alliance in the event of a global showdown and has
candidly admitted European dependence on American support. Even more significant is his prediction that by 1970
the West will still need the support of American nuclear
power, but it is Europe's dependence on American conventional arms that he expects will be reduced by then.[22]
The same thoughts were echoed by Premier Georges Pompidou in explaining to the National Assembly France's withdrawal from the NATO command:

> The agressor's certainty that he would sustain
> intolerable losses is the only guarantee that we
> can have against aggression. That is what justifies
> our own deterrent force. That is also what leads
> us to remain in the Atlantic alliance. . . . What
> has guaranteed peace is the alliance, insofar as it
> has brought to bear the threat of the American
> Strategic Air Command.[23]

If de Gaulle's policy rests on such an estimate, he is not far
removed from the American view favoring greater self-
reliance of European nations in conventional armaments.

The Chinese challenge to Moscow is probably more serious, inasmuch as China can exploit the animosities of the
peoples of Asia and Africa against the white race. However,
China's aspirations are checked by its present military
inferiority to the Soviet Union. It is noteworthy that none

of the communist countries of Eastern Europe, except for
Albania, have followed China's lead. Having become an
imperial power in its own right, China is saddled with all
the handicaps that such a position implies. But unlike the
Soviet Union, it cannot compensate for lost affection by
bestowing upon its would-be dependencies substantial
material benefits. It is little wonder, therefore, that when
communist leanings are closely connected with anti-Westernism or anti-Americanism, communist countries and
parties incline toward the powerful Soviet Union. Considerations of this nature account for the shift of North Korea
and North Vietnam to the Soviet side. Thus, one may conclude that China has been severely handicapped by its
feud with the Soviet Union. Its military development has
been seriously impaired by the withdrawal of Soviet technicians, industrial equipment, and up-to-date *matériel de
guerre*.

The hegemonial positions of the superpowers have been
further buttressed through economic aid programs, which
have been discussed in the preceding chapter. Such aid has
been given largely, though perhaps not exclusively, for political purposes, and the recipients have to perform in accordance with expectations. Suspensions of economic aid to
obstreperous allies and neutrals have occurred on both
sides. Even if such measures have been infrequent, they
have created insecurity for fear that aid may be stopped if
independence is pushed too far. Although such policies
have not been universally successful, the economic and
industrial preponderance of the Big Two has left its imprint
on hegemonial relations. The point is well illustrated by the
relations between the American continents in the West and
the economic organization of Eastern Europe on the Soviet
side. In spite of resistance to United States leadership,
South American leaders have repeatedly conceded the desirability of closer economic links to the United States. The
Colombian President has called for a special trade relationship between Latin America and the United States,[24] and
Latin American leaders are looking for United States' support of the establishment of a Latin American common
market.[25] Some of these proposals may not be cheerfully

received in Washington. They may actually imply the need for concessions that the United States is reluctant or unwilling to make, and may be deliberately designed to embarrass the United States. But they do reveal a special relationship between the Northern and Southern continents and the desire on the part of most major Latin American countries for a close attachment.

The Soviet Union has run into trouble with the economic organization it has established in Eastern Europe, the Council for Mutual Economic Assistance (COMECON). The Soviet Union has tried to combat the lack of cooperation of its allies by threatening to reduce its imports of machinery from Eastern Europe. The economic well-being of the area has largely depended on Soviet willingness to sell raw materials considerably below cost for the production of machinery. Were the Soviet Union to discontinue that practice and produce the machinery it needs itself, the Eastern European countries would find themselves in a serious economic predicament.[26] Such threats may not solve the existing difficulties within the organization, but they do show the great economic power wielded by the hegemonial country and the serious implications that this fact has for the political calculations of the allies. Nor can the significance of economic power be ignored in assessing the prospects of France and China breaking the hegemonial position of the leading powers. Third powers are acutely aware that desired protection and aid on any meaningful scale can only come from the superpowers, and that they presuppose smooth relations with them.

UNIQUENESS OF THE BIPOLAR ALLIANCES

The cold war alliances, then, present a curious paradox. Rigidity of alignment is combined with considerable vacillation in making and executing policy. Even weak nations have repeatedly been able to press their advantage by playing on the fears and sensibilities of the superpowers. Nevertheless, alliances are holding together today to a far greater extent than under the traditional multiple balance of power system, and, moreover, they show an appreciably greater susceptibility to guidance by the hegemonial powers. Allied defections to the opposing bloc have been rare and hardly merit the designation of a trend. Nor have repeated attempts by restive allies to create an independent third force been very successful. Certainly there is not, thus far, any serious indication that the world is returning to the traditional distribution of power. Regardless of advantages allies may be able to obtain, they may find it difficult to regain their independence. If they break away from their present association, they will have achieved little more than exchanging one master for another, and in the process they may very likely have incurred the wrath of both.

A further peculiarity of the bipolar alliances is their ambitious plan to provide not only for military cooperation but also for cooperation in the political, economic, and cultural spheres. The tactical importance of ideologies has tempted the hegemonial powers to take an interest, and frequently to become a force, in their allies' domestic affairs by supporting political stability or bringing about political changes by reforming internal economies or reducing the rate of illiteracy of allied peoples. This state of affairs is not likely to change as long as the Big Two retain a clear superiority in destructive weapons. They will be able to do this for some time, in spite of the efforts made by third powers in the nuclear and missile realms. To be sure, minor nuclear establishments will soon be able to cause severe damage and may create a serious disturbance in international relations; their ability to devastate continents, however, is not as yet to be anticipated.

CHAPTER SIX

THE NONALIGNED

THE PERSISTENCE OF NATIONALISM

The most obvious objection that can be raised against the bipolar thesis is the continued presence of third "powers" that have managed with some success to pursue their own national interests. In fact, the number of new states has risen sharply since the end of the Second World War, and the impassioned proclamations of independence by their governments have created the impression that the era of the sovereign state is just about to reach its zenith. Preoccupied with their material well-being, these new states have put the world on notice that they wish to remain aloof from the global conflict. This desire certainly is a factor to be reckoned with, especially since the upsurge of nationalistic passions has enabled the nation-state to evoke unprecedently strong affections. Nationalism has a particularly strong hold over those who have only recently attained independence. Its impact has not been diminished by the fact that in many new areas the transition from tribal fragmentation to national unity has yet to be made.

The nationalistic commitments of the third powers in many ways seem tainted with anachronism. Objectively, the sovereign state and the state system no longer make much sense. Both political and technological developments in recent decades have surpassed the state as an effective military unit and have left the semi-global bloc as the only type of political organization with enough viability to secure its existence. This ability, based on military, industrial, and economic strength, is sufficiently unique to distinguish sharply the two blocs from other powers. Although the state system still exists and continues to make an imprint on international politics, it is difficult to evaluate the impact made by third states. It is the purpose of this chapter to examine the position of the nonaligned countries.

SUPERPOWER PERSPECTIVES

The concern of the superpowers for the uncommitted countries and their willingness to adapt their policies, where possible, to the latters' needs has been explained in the preceding chapter. The disproportionate influence that the uncommitted have been able to exert has been less easy to explain. This is all the more surprising in view of the general disfavor with which the Big Two have looked upon noncommitment. Almost from the outset, both powers have brought pressure to bear upon the nonaligned nations to join their respective alliance systems, and have heaped moral condemnation on those who have resisted. In the case of the Soviet Union, ideological reasons can easily be found to explain such intolerance: The two-fold division of humanity, germane to Marxian thought, makes no provision for third groupings and envisages as inescapable the eventual alignment of all men with one or the other side. Moreover, confident knowledge of the future course of history imposes the moral obligation to accelerate progress by actively supporting the "exploited" in their struggle with the "exploiters." This line of thinking has persisted in the more advanced phases of Soviet ideological development as indicated by Stalin's pronouncement, shortly after the end of the Second World War, that neither the wartime alliance nor the common search for an enduring peace could possibly prevent the showdown between the two camps.

American ideological thinking also tends to censure neutrals on moral grounds. Although the concept of the universal brotherhood of men is contrary to the division of humanity into two camps, such logic has been of small effect in actual practice. Devotion to the construction of a world in which people can live free from fear of political oppression easily leads to intolerance of those not inclined toward following the example set by the United States. The ideological fervor is accentuated by bipolarism. Whereas the pluralism characteristic of other configurations of international politics tends to temper the salvationist zeal engendered by universalist ideologies, the usual restraints remain ineffectual in bipolar politics. On the contrary, the nature of the political struggle tends to reinforce the ideological division. The temptation is almost irresistible to look upon the dualist contest as a showdown between the forces of good and evil. The sincere, if erroneous, belief that the clash is a moral one seems to justify classifying all humanity in terms of obtuse friend-enemy categories. Failing to discharge his moral obligations toward the righteous side, the neutral incurs the wrath of both parties. It is a common human failing in a showdown of such apparent simplicity as the bipolar one to regard as an enemy him who refuses to be a friend.

Despite their initial indignation, both the United States and the Soviet Union soon began to assume a less moralizing tone. In fact, since the early 1950's, their policies toward the nonaligned have undergone a notable change. Since that time, they have tried to outdo each other in supporting neutralist trends. To win the sympathies of uncommitted countries, both President Eisenhower and Chairman Khrushchev undertook extensive goodwill tours in 1959 and 1960. For the United States, this change marked a special departure from its well-known penchant for moralistic foreign policies. Some peculiar virtue seemed to have been rediscovered in neutrality, which was a commonplace position in this country's early history. Both sides have been particularly attentive to the newly emerging neutrals overseas and have generously provided them with economic and military aid. Some have received aid from the United

States, others from the Soviet Union, and still others, such as India, Cambodia, and Indonesia, from both sides. The case of India is particularly revealing. President Kennedy went on record praising the virtue of India's neutralism. Thus, in its border war with China, India not only received help from the United States, much to the dismay of Pakistan, but from the Soviet Union, despite the latter's alliance with China. Also of interest has been the American relationship with Yugoslavia. The United States has given aid to Yugoslavia to strengthen its independence of the Soviet Union, while avoiding any serious attempt to draw the recipient into the Western alliance.

Although it has become fashionable to support neutrals, their anomalous status in the bipolar order requires an examination of the superpowers' political motives. The political rationale is not hard to discover. The remoteness of open warfare in face of the nuclear stalemate and the concomitant depreciation of power blocs has forced the superpowers to accept the cold war as a permanent condition. But the need for flexibility in political warfare is no sure indication that their basic hostility toward nonalignment has actually been abandoned. Although in the eyes of the rest of the world neutrality has become a progressively respectable status, the superpowers have come to view the actions of the uncommitted increasingly in terms of political expediency.

The practical necessity to support neutralist aspirations of the nonaligned has not, to be sure, been able to silence American moralizing. The frequent unwillingness of ex-colonials to let themselves be integrated into an alliance with their former colonial masters has caused considerable moral indignation in the West. Even though the most that could practically be accomplished was to keep the uncommitted in a state of benevolent neutrality, there have been recurrent expressions of American moral indignation. In 1956, Secretary of State Dulles openly branded neutrality as "an immoral and short-sighted conception." In the summer of 1962, Secretary Rusk expressed similar sentiments to the House Foreign Affairs Committee at a closed meeting when he said, "The picture of the world revolution offered by the communist countries and the more revolutionary and far more attractive picture sketched out in the charter of the United Nations. . . . On that issue, there can be no neutrality for independent nations." [1] A similar disdain for neutrals was expressed in the spring of 1963 by former Vice President Richard M. Nixon, who, in addressing the American Society of Newspaper Editors, said, "We should have respect for the right of any nation to be neutral, but in developing the defense and foreign policies of the United States we should remember that if it were not for the power of the United States, no nation in the world today could enjoy the *luxury of neutrality*." (Italics mine.) [2]

The sincerity of Soviet proneutralist policy is equally subject to suspicion. Despite their apparent commitment to the attainment of ideological goals, their policy has been characterized by an extraordinary pragmatism in tactical matters. In fact, their encouragement of the extreme nationalism that has emerged in underdeveloped and recently emancipated countries has been a useful means of drawing the latter away from the West. The inherent hostility of Marxian thought to nationalism has not deterred the Soviet Union from supporting such strategically useful tendencies, thereby adding fuel to the resentments of colonials against Western imperialism.

The opportunistic nature of the American and Soviet attitudes toward the unaligned has been confirmed with the passage of time. It has become increasingly obvious that the superpowers are more vitally interested in bringing as many neutrals as possible over to their side than in helping them solidify their independence. To be sure, economic and technical aid, especially if it is of a nonpolitical and nonmilitary nature, may appear innocent. But even if aid is given in a generous spirit, the donor cannot but hope to buy with it at least the assurance that the recipient will remain impervious to the pressures and lures of the opponent. As a matter of fact, American aid has been largely reserved to nations friendly to the United States. The Soviet Union has loudly denied that political strings of any kind are attached to its aid and has prided itself on emphasizing trade with, rather than aid to, unaligned, underdeveloped nations as proof of its sincerity and disinterest. Such claims may appear plausible at first sight, but on closer inspection, they turn out to be deceptive. Although the relations between donor and recipient, buyer and supplier, seldom are simple and unambiguous, it is rare that economic ties between strong and weak nations do not imply at least a dominating influence of the stronger party. Economic aid in any form will furnish a potent lever for influencing foreign policy, and possibly also internal politics. An example is the repeated economic squeezes the United States has applied on the Congo. In 1962, it tried to boycott Tshombe's Katanga, to force his joining the Congolese federation, with the hope that political unity would deter the Soviet Union from establishing a relationship in the area.[3] And in the summer of 1963, some portion of American aid was suspended to force Premier Adoula to undertake reforms that would render aid more effective.[4]

Economic aid has not, of course, been uniformly effective. In some instances, the United States has found its most sincere and generous efforts to help newly rising nations poorly rewarded. Anti-Western sentiments have made former colonials lean toward the Soviet Union, despite Western aid or the superior Western claims of truth, justice, and peace. Frequently, too, the breakdown of traditional patterns in the wake of economic development has created fear and discontent among those uprooted by Western civilization, thus leaving the door wide open to communism. Especially annoying to the United States has been the possibility of being caught up in others' hostilities, such as that between Pakistan and India, or the Arab states and Israel, with the likely result of making enemies of both nations. In such situations, the United States has had no choice but to accept its setbacks gracefully. Abandoning foreign aid has not been a practical possibility. If the opponent has a foreign aid program, withdrawal of American aid would be tantamount to a withdrawal from the competition. Support even of undesirable governments has seemed preferable to a collapse of established regimes, which would leave the countries in question exposed to total and immediate communist takeovers. It may be a consolation that the Soviet Union has experienced similar disappointments. Its enormous investments in neutral countries have frequently yielded meager political returns.

Attacks upon neutralism have not been confined to such subtle methods as economic penetration. In addition to economic ties, ideological methods, especially popular with the Soviet Union, have often been effective. This is pointed up in some papers presented by Soviet scholars at the Ghana conference of "Africanists" in 1962; these papers were obviously designed to please the Africans rather than to contribute to the enlightenment of fellow scholars.[5] Such an opportunity to promote public relations was not to be lost in the intricacies of scholarly debate. In a similar vein, the Soviet Union won a major victory when it succeeded in persuading the government of Kenya in 1963 to let it set up a government news agency to function as the main source of news for the country. The plan was that Tass and the Czechoslovak news agency Ceteka would provide a daily service of international news, while the agency itself would be operated by communist-trained African journalists and technicians.[6] American attempts to establish political bridgeheads in Africa have followed similar lines. Rather than trying to enlist the newcomers as members in its alliance system, the United States has encouraged democratic institutions wherever possible, hopeful that these would provide a basis for closer relations with the West.

The inordinate concern of powers of such military preponderance as the United States and the Soviet Union with the unaligned may seem strange, but, as in the case of the allies, it has a rational basis. What seems more remarkable is the caution with which the superpowers have sought to attain their goals and the variation in their efforts in different areas. The interest of the Big Two is not equally pronounced with reference to all neutrals. For example, both have shown a relative indifference toward the nonaligned nations of Central Europe. The Soviet Union, apparently, has considered it impolitic to encroach upon Sweden, Austria, and Switzerland, which by inclination and tradition lean on the West both economically and politically. Any Soviet attempt to bring them into the communist fold would necesarily provoke military pressure or action, and thus produce the acute danger of a clash with the United States. In turn, the United States sees little advantage in integrating these same countries into its alliance system. The political cost of pressuring them into a formal association would outweigh the advantages of such an association. The only conceivable benefit the United States might expect would be the satisfaction of expanding the sphere of its ideology.

Removed from the static conditions prevailing along the dividing lines between the two worlds, the unaligned countries in peripheral areas provide more scope for cold war competition. Such countries, comparable in political importance to many of the committed nations, are the objects of attention to a degree that seems vastly out of proportion to their actual or potential military strength. The fact that they are not formally associated with one side or the other is no indication that they are not relevant to the cold war. Normally some practical reasons can be found to explain the failure of the superpowers to draw them into a closer relationship. In some instances, formal association is not possible, in others it would involve the assumption of too great a liability to make it desirable. This does not mean that those who cannot be enlisted as allies are not fit objects of solicitation. Strict impartiality is favored by neither side, and neutralist tendencies appear worth fostering only when chances of conversion are remote or promise to be too costly. In that case, neutrality can adequately serve the purpose of frustrating the opponent's expansionist designs. This may explain the interest of the United States in the integrity of the unaligned countries in Africa and Asia, where the unfortunate position of the Western imperialist powers has left no alternative. In view of the strong anti-Western sentiments, any policy other than neutralism would drive these new nations into alliance with the Soviet Union or China. The Soviet Union, too, has had to tread cautiously and has confined itself to building up its prestige and good will in underdeveloped areas. In addition to creating a barrier against the advances of an aggressive opponent the support of neutralism can loosen the opponent's alliances, as American support of neutralist leanings in Yugoslavia has shown.

Interestingly enough, the anomaly of neutral status has not prevented the superpowers from attempting to neutralize certain areas. It is necessary, however, to remember that the areas involved have presented atypical situations. In the case of Austria, neutralization was made possible by a coincidence of the interests of the Big Two, who seem to have judged the country too insignificant strategically and politically to make it an object of competition. Antarctica's neutralization reflects no change of the international political pattern; the area is of no conceivable use to anyone today and does not promise to become any more desirable in the future.

The neutralization of Indochina, at first sight, appears surprising, since the area has been of much interest to both superpowers. Although Laos was neutralized following the division of the Kingdom in 1954 with the approval of both the Soviet Union and the United States, their respect for the country's neutrality was less than impressive. The American strategy between 1957 and 1960 to influence Laotian policy was hardly in keeping with the spirit of the agreement. The result was renewed internal strife between communist and anticommunist forces. Since then, communism has made steady progress in Laos. Not only have the communist guerrillas been able to enlarge their conquest, but the Western-backed government, enjoying only feeble popular support, was forced to yield to a coalition in which the communists hold an equal share with the pro-Western and the neutralist factions. A further attempt was made to ensure Laotian neutrality through the *Fourteen-Nation Declaration and Protocol on Neutrality in Laos* signed in Geneva on July 23, 1962. In that declaration, the participating powers undertook to respect the neutrality of Laos by refraining from all attempts to bring the area into any military alliance, and from interfering directly or indirectly in the country's internal affairs, as well as by cooperating in keeping the country free from all foreign troops. The International Commission for Supervision and Control, set up in 1954 and composed of representatives of Canada, India, and Poland, was entrusted with supervising the execution of the protocol's provisions. The agreement has not been able to prevent a progressive Eastward orientation. It has neither brought the civil war to an end, stopped Soviet foreign aid, nor made the government forget its geographic proximity to the Chinese colossus. Due to its strategic position in relation to Vietnam, Laos has become a focus of tension and a theater of silent war betwen the United States and Asian communism.[7]

There may be merit in the American charge that the activities of the opposing camp have violated the Geneva Protocol. But it was probably inevitable that under such an agreement Laos would advance along the road to communism. Once the country was neutralized and a coalition government established with communist participation, native communists could complete the job. The local strength of communism and the lack of equally strong anticommunist forces could not but turn neutrality in favor of the communist powers. A genuine neutralization of the whole area of Indochina, as proposed by President de Gaulle, that provided for the withdrawal of all outsiders, very likely would work against the United States. If the countries involved were left to their own devices, a communist takeover via the internal political process could be expected to follow. When the fighting was resumed in the spring of 1963, the American government reminded the Soviet government of its obligations, and urged it to use its influence to stop the fighting. Although Khrushchev did not indicate that he would or could restrain the communist forces in Laos, Averell Harriman, sent to Moscow by President Kennedy to negotiate the issue, insisted that Laos was "a symbol whether the two countries can work together to achieve mutually agreed upon results." [8]

The lesson to be learned from the attempted neutralization of Laos is that big power cooperation is not hopeful when both sides have vital interests in an area. Chances that a basis for mutual accommodation can be found are not enhanced by the discord between the Soviet Union and China and the undisguised preference of the United States for Soviet control. Neutralization seems to be possible only if the area concerned is of no interest to either side, or if its neutralization is of equal advantage to both. It was, therefore, entirely logical for President Kennedy to turn to Chairman Khrushchev to negotiate a cease-fire in Laos, although no Soviet armed forces were involved in the fighting.

NEUTRALIST PERSPECTIVES

Thus far cold war neutralism has been considered from the vantage point of the big powers. But how does the world look from the perspective of the uncommitted? What are their aspirations? What distinguishes them from the aligned? And in what way can they be compared to neutrals in the technical legal sense?

The reasons for nonalignment are complex, and they are different for the old countries and the new nations. But despite variations in degree, from the impartiality of Switzerland to the close association of Indonesia with China before the change in September 1965, the basic common denominator is the refusal of a firm commitment to either of the two blocs. However, this is as far as the detachment of the uncommitted states goes, and to appraise their position and their role in the bipolar world, it is essential to observe the wide gulf that separates them from the position of neutrals under international law in open war. Legal neutrality rests on the acknowledgment of special rights of the belligerents, and imposes upon neutrals the obligation of impartiality in thought and action. In nonalignment the relationship is reversed; the unaligned refuse to recognize that the contesting parties in the cold war have any special rights, and insist on their own rights regardless of the interests of the contenders. Moreover, noncommitment does not signify indifference or nonparticipation, and in reality, the uncommitted normally take sides when cold war issues arise. Most of them are neither morally or politically indifferent toward the power contest nor likely to think of themselves as disinterested spectators. They are quick to take a part in world politics and to attempt to influence the superpowers. They feel particularly equipped to do this since, in

keeping a free hand, they can deal with cold war issues on
the basis of merit rather than of commitment.

The role played by the uncommitted in cold war politics,
as well as their decision to remain unaligned, is partly determined by sympathies and a sense of obligation. By playing the role of mediators in issues between the big powers,
they feel that they can make a significant contribution to
the avoidance of a general war and the concomitant destruction of all humanity, or that they can help prevent the
rise of a world dictatorship by one power. A statement by
Sékou Touré perhaps expresses the role that the newly
rising world of Asia and Africa—constituting the bulk of
the unaligned—envisages for itself:

> African neutralism, then, is not shameful indif-
> ference, a sort of political demobilization. On
> the contrary, it is the expression of a lively
> faith in a happy future for mankind. It is some-
> thing active, a participating force, an active
> agent in the struggle for the achievement of
> a world society—emancipated, fraternal and
> united.[9]

Such general humanitarian aspirations are sufficiently
vague to form the basis of a universally acceptable program. But translated into specifics, the pragmatic basis of
neutralism becomes increasingly apparent. The position of
unaligned countries largely depends on an appraisal of their
particular interests. Their most urgent desire is to maintain
independence in shaping their own future. Self-determination of their fate implies, above all, the ability to stay out of
a war between the major powers. The realization of that
goal would be clearly jeopardized by alignment, which frequently works to provoke the other side. The Africans, in
particular, have resisted alignment for fear that the competition of the big powers would divide the continent into
two parts, thereby seriously undermining their strength. A
further consideration is the desire to modernize their societies, and, to that end, most of the unaligned desperately
need the kind of economic and technological aid that the

superpowers can provide to a satisfactory measure. Such needs are more likely to be satisfied through participation than through a policy of nonparticipation.

In some ways, the bipolar system actually favors the unaligned. The rivalry of the Big Two and their competition for the favor of the lesser powers provide the latter with considerable opportunity for self-assertion and even for an active part in world politics. It has not been uncommon for them to defy the Big Two, as well as other major powers. For example, Indonesia, when it was still leaning strongly toward communism, entered into alliance with Malaya and the Philippines, two of the most pro-Western countries in Asia, in defiance of Chinese pressures. Taking advantage of the Sino-Soviet rift, a small neighbor was thus able to challenge Chinese aspirations to establish a hegemony over Asia.[10] Perhaps the most glaring defiance of a big power by a small nation was the expulsion by the Congolese government of the entire Soviet diplomatic mission because of alleged subversive activities.[11] Even in areas where communism and nationalism have joined forces and interests run parallel, the Soviet Union has frequently found it difficult, if not impossible, to give political direction.[12] In a similar vein, political maneuvers have, at times, enabled Tito to play himself off as one of the world's leading statesmen and to exert a significant influence. He was accorded warm receptions and shown unusual respect during his tour of Latin America, and his call for economic and political independence of the great blocs evoked wide acclaim. Moreover, during his alienation from the Soviet Union, Tito was able to resist becoming an American ally in spite of his reliance on American help.

Native elites have also been successful in using neutralism as a means of extracting economic and military aid from both the United States and the Soviet Union without assuming definite political commitments. In their eagerness to improve their strategic position in the cold war, both superpowers have responded generously. Many cases could be cited, but a few will illustrate the point. Before the events of June 1967 Nasser played the United States against the Soviet Union without assuming a definite commitment, and he was more successful in exploiting the Russians than the Russians were in exploiting him. The extensive military and economic aid received from the Soviet Union for over a decade did not deter Egypt from outlawing the Communist Party, or from accepting American aid. At the same time, American aid has prevented neither Egypt nor other recipients, such as Pakistan and Indonesia, from openly censuring the United States. Similarly, the Burmese government accepting aid from both the United States and China has remained cool to the West, despite its dependence on American aid.[13] After the Chinese attack, India was able to obtain military aid from both superpowers without committing itself to either.[14]

If these few episodes exemplify the neutrals' strength and independence, the record also reveals the tenuous basis of their autonomy. Nehru's long-cherished dream of non-alignment was brutally shattered by China's attack on his country. His contention that it was only "a compulsion of events which has made us accept Western military aid" [15] was but a feeble attempt to cover up the bankruptcy of his independent policy. In time, India has come to lean heavily on the United States and the Soviet Union for defense against China. In this case, the close relations have not necessarily meant siding with one against the other inasmuch as American and Soviet interest coincide to an appreciable extent. However, India has gravitated more toward the American side since the United States alone can provide the needed economic and technical assistance. In any event, India's international independence has given way to alignment with the great European powers against China. Its bilateral dependence may well change into unilateral alignment with the West if and when its policies become incompatible with Soviet efforts to maintain hegemony in the communist world. Tito's claims of independence are no more valid. His words and actions have providentially fallen in line with Soviet policy. While stressing his continued friendship for the United States, his views on Berlin, Laos, Cuba, and the armament contest have been almost indistinguishable from those of the Soviets. Finland, too, in spite of its neutrality and pro-Western orientation, has had to make strategic and military concessions to the Soviet Union.

Such vacillations are hardly compelling evidence of independence. In fact, they show more clearly that such countries, in spite of their unaligned status, lean at any given moment on either one or the other bloc. Only if they feel protected by one big power will they dare challenge the opposing big power. Characteristically, Cambodia's warning that it would repel American military encroachments was coupled with the assertion that it was being backed by China.[16] Moreover, it was not by accident that the Cambodian militancy vis-à-vis the United States lost momentum with the increasing frequency of American military successes in Vietnam and the diminishing probability of tangible Chinese protection. In the last analysis, all the small nations continue to seek the protection of one or both major powers. Interestingly enough, the South Vietnamese government strongly opposed a neutralist solution of its internal difficulties.[17] The Thai government, notwithstanding its irritation with United States' increased military aid to Cambodia, continued to stress its ties with the West because of their vital importance for the protection of its "sovereignty and independence." [18] Even Ireland has shown an anxiousness in recent years to integrate itself into Europe and to forsake the myth of neutrality. And Mr. Bourguiba candidly admitted the tenuous nature of Tunisia's sovereign status by suggesting to Secretary Rusk in 1961, in his appeal for American help, that "the free world act before another world does." [19]

It is this need of support that the superpowers hope to exploit for their own ends. The Soviet Union has been particularly skillful in this respect, and only too often neutralism or neutralization has been preparatory to a communist takeover. Few neutrals have any illusions concerning the motives of their benefactors. But if they have avoided a firm commitment in order to realize their own aspirations, they have been highly susceptible to the influences of those who are most helpful in bringing about this realization. Ideally, they would, no doubt, prefer to receive support from both sides since this would assure them the maximum freedom of action. However, in practice they find it difficult to maintain an exact balance and become increasingly susceptible to the pressures brought to bear by the side promising the more rewarding association.[20]

NEUTRALISTS AS A THIRD FORCE

The crucial question in appraising the role of the unaligned is the kind and extent of influence they can exert. During the past decade, attempts have been made to create a "neutralist bloc" or "third force" to play a decisive part in world politics, independent of the great power blocs in the East and West. It was hoped that a united front of the unaligned could become a significant force. Such endeavors have foundered on a lack of unity resulting from a great diversity of interests. The Cairo Conference of neutralist states in the fall of 1964 revealed a wide split. Considering the heterogeneous nature of the group, composed as it is of developed, semideveloped, and underdeveloped countries, and comprising old powers, semicolonials, and emerging states, the lack of unity is understandable.

Those least interested in concerted action are the unaligned of Europe, and, in fact, Finland was the only European country represented. The conference also showed considerable differences in the neutralism of the participants. Some were highly independent, others seemed unaligned in name only. The newly emerged states in Africa and Asia frequently claimed to be fighting for certain common causes, but found it difficult to agree on just who was the enemy. Some took a stand against Western colonialism, others were opposed to communist imperialism; some appeared to be seeking the destruction of capitalism, others were chiefly concerned with the threat of war.

Although a moderate group led by India and Yugoslavia believed that it could play a useful part in minimizing cold war tensions, the outlook of the majority was more parochial and did not go far beyond their immediate national concerns. Political instability, primitive political forms, clashing interests, and mutual hatreds are problems of sufficient complexity to preclude sustained unity. It is doubt-

ful that the threat to human survival is felt to be of sufficient urgency to subordinate existing animosities to the need
for harmony. Domestic and immediate problems are usually
closer to the hearts of people than dangers of East-West
confrontation.

The newly emerging world, in particular, presents a picture of disunity and diversity of interests. Asia is torn by
fears and aspirations: fear of the hegemonial ambitions of
China, resisted by some, welcomed by others, and accepted
with resignation by still others; fear of being overwhelmed
by the large number of new African states, which has led
the noncommunist states of Asia to form the Asian and
Pacific Council; particularistic aspirations of independence
and rapidly increasing well-being. Even the relatively
modest project of launching the Malaysian Federation
almost collapsed due to the last minute balking of the
government of Brunei, and it was further endangered by
Indonesian opposition to an allegedly neocolonialist British
venture. The Middle East has always been torn by strife,
and not even a common hostility to Israel had been able to
bring the Arab states into an effective union. There has also
been great concern with the Balkanization of the African
continent, and the new Pan-African movement cannot yet
boast tangible political achievements. Although these difficulties may eventually be overcome, this is not likely to
happen soon. Even the modest attempt to form a fragmen-
tary East African union has run into serious difficulties,[21]
and the cohesion of any political unit transcending the
tribal level remains problematical. African nationhood, following, as it does, the territorial lines marked out by colonial masters to accommodate their own political con-
venience, is artificial and has little meaning to people whose
prime loyalties are to tribal organizations. It can be expected that the disunity of the unaligned will increase as
their number grows.

In view of the lack of agreement, it seems euphemistic to
speak of a "bloc of the unaligned." The Cairo Conference
failed to produce a redefinition of the role of the unaligned.
Wanting in purpose, and vastly outdistanced militarily by
the great powers, the noncommitted, as their helplessness in

the Cuban missile crisis has shown, are not a force that can function as a balancer and cannot possibly intercede in the event of a showdown between the Big Two. Their desire for independent power must remain unfulfilled under present conditions.

It is often argued that even in the absence of an effective third force, the unaligned can be constructive in easing cold war tensions. They can contribute by making mediation possible, and by keeping the channels of communication open. The moderating effect that this could have upon the cold war certainly is not to be denied. However, it does not obviate the limitations that their military inferiority imposes upon them. They do not possess the power needed to manipulate the balance to prevent a military clash between the Big Two, and the fate of humanity continues to rest in the latters' hands. There is little they can do to force a settlement of disputes in which the big powers are involved. The Korean conflict was terminated by the United States when it was ready, with little reference to the unaligned states. Nor have third states been able to bring about a settlement in Vietnam, and though an all-Asian conference has been proposed to deal with the problem, it seems unlikely that, even if the plan were to materialize, it would produce any tangible results. The fact remains that no combination of third states has the power to resolve the basic predicament underlying the cold war, that is, the irreducible fear and mutual suspicion of the Big Two, which are the bases of continuing tensions.

The military facts are undeniable. However, the questions must be raised whether they will continue to be relevant at a time of relaxed tensions and what effect will the softening of the cold war have upon the part that may be played by the unaligned. No doubt the present trend away from power blocs and the impact of nuclear weapons have enhanced the possibility of adjustment and depreciated power in international politics. There has, consequently, been increased scope for manipulation and mediation, and this has provided the unaligned with the opportunity for effective participation. At the same time, the role of the mediator has become less vital as the cold war has lessened in intensity. The profound desire of the Big Two to avoid open conflict has caused them to act slowly and deliberately, thereby reducing the need for mediation. The chief remaining danger is the possibility of an insolvable predicament. In such an event, the unaligned will very likely not be of great help—on the one hand, because they are not strong enough to act as balancers, and on the other, because the heightened mutual distrust of the Big Two will not be overcome through mediation.

Another problem that has hampered the effective intercession of the unaligned states is the attenuation of the line between the aligned and the unaligned resulting from the relaxation of the cold war. The loosening of the alliance systems in the coexistence phase of the cold war has ended the monopoly of the unaligned on independent action in the international political process; they normally have to share the glory with some of the aligned states. The result has been the assumption, to an appreciable extent, of the functions of the unaligned by aligned states, which have greater influence because of their association with the superpowers. The new nations, forming the bulk of the unaligned, have been further handicapped by their failure to appreciate the sense of urgency that the choice between "freedom" and "communism" has for the older nations. Their absorption in the tasks of ending imperialism and building their countries has alienated them from the West and has brought them closer to the communist bloc, depriving them of the advantages which noncommitment affords.

THE UNITED NATIONS AND NEUTRALISM

The belief of the unaligned that they can play an effective part in world politics largely rests on a concept of power based on numbers in the United Nations. To evaluate the soundness of that expectation, two questions must be raised: first, what is the role of the United Nations in contemporary world politics; and second, what influence have the unaligned had upon the activities of the United Nations and, through that organization, on world politics?

Compared with the intentions of the founders, the func-

tion of the United Nations has undergone an appreciable
transformation. The founders were realistic enough not to
set up a comprehensive security organization. Paying their
respect to the vast gap between great and small powers that
had resulted from the Second World War, they provided
an enforcement apparatus to cope with aggressiveness on
the part of small states that was to rest on agreement between the big powers. This endeavor to ensure world peace
by making the big powers, and particularly the Big Two,
the guarantors of the existing order was doomed from the
outset. Little security is obtained by settling small power
conflicts as long as it is impossible to restrain the Big Two.
But even in the realm of small power conflicts, the effectiveness of the organization has been sharply reduced by
the involvement of Big Two interests in most of these
disputes.

Despite the modest goals of the founding fathers, as reflected in the Charter, the United Nations seemed to be
gaining unexpected strength during the first decade of its
existence and even attempted, as in the case of Korea, to
function as a collective security organization, although this
experience was anything but encouraging. The expansion
of the organization's activity was made possible through
the fortuitous support of the United States by a two-thirds
majority in the General Assembly. The change in compo-
sition resulting from the admission since 1955 of the emergent states has deprived the United States of dependable
majority support; during the second decade, the Secretary-
General repeatedly sounded a pessimistic note that the
United Nations was increasingly being bypassed in matters
having a crucial bearing on world peace.[22] Such frustrations seem borne out by the failure of the powers to put
the Vietnam problem squarely to the United Nations. But
it must be remembered that this is the kind of problem
for which the Charter paralyzes the organization by means
of the veto.

If the United Nations was to survive the evanescence
of the premises on which it rested, it had to find a sphere
of activity other than the prevention and termination of
war through collective action. In this it has been sufficiently

successful to justify its continued existence. While the organization has not been able to stave off even little wars, it has been instrumental in limiting a number of them, and in isolating some from cold war politics through preventive diplomacy. A good illustration of United Nations effectiveness is its action in the Congo; by filling a power vacuum it protected the area against becoming the arena of contest between the Big Two. Although it is far from clear that United Nations forces were able to provide a solid basis for orderly government, they helped prevent intervention by the big powers. The organization has also been useful in providing a forum for discussion in international crises and in clearing the road to a smoother transition in the liquidation of colonialism. An interesting development is the new role that the United Nations seems to have acquired without much fanfare. Through investigation and assessment Secretary General U Thant was of considerable help, without any specific authorization or means of enforcement, in clearing the road to the inclusion of Borneo and Sarawak in the Federation of Malaysia, despite the objections of Indonesia.[23]

This transformation of functions was substantially helped along by the unaligned. Moreover, the unaligned are increasingly setting the tone of the world organization. Their presence has been helpful in many ways. The enthusiasm with which they have inspired the United Nations has been refreshing and has imbued the organization with renewed vigor. Through their participation, too, the United Nations has been able to exert a restraining influence on the Big Two. The basis for that influence has been the psychopolitical nature of the cold war. Both superpowers have attempted to use the United Nations as a forum for their propaganda, and this has opened the door to the influence of the unaligned. The use that the Big Two have made of the United Nations has again been illustrated by the Vietnam issue. Their peace proposals were designed to make a favorable impression on world opinion rather than to find a solution. But the importance the big powers have attached to propaganda as an instrument of international strategy has made them extraordinarily sensitive to world opinion and they are anxious to adapt their policies more closely to the mood of the rest of the world. Probably the chief contribution of the unaligned to the United Nations has been to steer the organization away from its former heavy orientation toward the Western side, bringing it more closely in line with the present political and military balance between the two blocs. Thus, they have reduced the chances of a walk-out by one of the Big Two, which could occur if one finds itself permanently outvoted. However, the degree of influence that the new states have gained in world politics and the effect that they have had upon the role of the United Nations are questions of a different order.

If the United Nations has been ineffectual in settling disputes, it has contributed to a *détente* in other ways. One important service it has performed has been to provide the initiative for settlements, as was the case in the Berlin and Korean crises. The United Nations has also been useful as a framework for negotiations and as a face-saving device. Some of the neutralist states have played an important part in all this. But if they have strengthened the United Nations by making it more representative and by increasing its longevity, they have also weakened it by trying to use the organization for their own purposes. In fact, in his annual report of 1967 the Secretary-General recommended, to avoid a further weakening of the organization, that the General Assembly discourage the future admission of very small states unable to assume full financial and political obligations.[24] The United Nations has been useful to them by providing a forum from which those who might otherwise find it difficult can make themselves heard. Moreover, if the new states are in need of support, it is far safer and less costly, in terms of diminished independence, to lean on the United Nations than on one of the big powers. But their preoccupation with particular problems has created considerable disunity in the councils of the United Nations. Increasing divisions have developed between the Asian and African countries, and there has been considerable dissension within the Asian and African groups. So divided, the unaligned have had a less decisive influence both inside and outside the United Nations than they might have had.

A special difficulty arising from the particular concerns of the new states is the predominance of the colonial issue in United Nations debates. The apparent result has been a tendency to crowd out basic cold war issues. Reportedly, the Africans, in particular, have monopolized debate with their own problems, to the point of preventing any serious discussion of such vital matters as Vietnam, nuclear weapons, and a space treaty, with the result of driving the representatives of other countries from the General Assembly chamber.[25] This is not to say that colonialism has not been important in the cold war; the underdeveloped world has been an arena of the East-West conflict, and the Big Two have repeatedly been forced to take a stand on colonial issues. Both have had no choice but to defer to this new force, as their support of African claims in the United Nations shows. But it must also be remembered that, to the extent to which the colonial issue has a direct bearing on the cold war, the countries involved are objects rather than subjects of the policies of the great powers, which hardly places them in a position to act as suitable mediators. It has been contended that the involvement of the underdeveloped countries in the pursuit of their own interests has served to cushion the big power controversy. This contention is subject to question. The emotionalism aroused by the colonial issue has introduced considerable bitterness into United Nations debates. Moreover, it has frequently forced the United States and the Soviet Union to take opposing positions and, if anything, has increased tensions.

The failure to create an effective balancing force cannot, of course, simply be blamed on the political inadequacy of the unaligned. Neither they nor the United Nations have the power to reduce tensions between the superpowers or to prevent conflict when vital interests of the big powers clash. It has been contended, and rightly so, that the proper function of the United Nations is to "improve and stabilize the working of the balance of power system," rather than to provide a collective security system capable of dealing with disputes arising between the Big Two.[26] But since the present balance of power is essentially a balance between the two camps, the United Nations must reflect that balance. The record clearly shows that in the absence of great power agreement, positive action by the United Nations has depended on the acquiescence of these powers. This also means that regardless of the role played by the unaligned, the issues between the superpowers are more likely to be settled directly by them than through the United Nations. In fact, neither the United Nations nor the unaligned had any influence on the settlement of the Cuban crisis of 1962, even though the United Nations was the formal setting for the negotiations. Nor was the United Nations involved in the coexistence debate. The disarmament issue also exemplifies the bilateralism of world politics. Although the disarmament committee has included Asian, African, and Latin American states, the superpowers have kept the issues firmly in hand throughout. Needless to say, under present conditions there can be no disarmament or armament limitation without substantial agreement between the United States and the Soviet Union.

All this is not to detract from the eminently useful role that the United Nations plays. As a forum of world public opinion, it has tended to restrain the big powers, since the political nature of the power contest has made both exceedingly sensitive to criticism. Moreover, cold war politics make it appear inexpedient for them to withdraw from it. Not only would withdrawal lose them the respect of the rest of the world, it would also be a self-denial of any influence they can now exert through the United Nations by participating in and directing matters of global concern. This consideration has become especially important since the loosening of alignments and commitments.

These vital contributions cannot, of course, obscure the dependence of the future of the world on the Big Two. The relative stabilization of coexistence and the easing of cold war tensions are the result of the terrifying dimensions of contemporary armaments technology, rather than of the activities of the United Nations. This dependence on technological conditions is likely to increase as the Big Two forge ahead in developing implements of destruction. As the cold war fronts have become less clearly defined and the contest has expanded in scope, the interests of the contestants have become universal and their influence ubiquitous. In local conflicts, too, influence of the big powers is felt. In the clash between India and China both sides received aid; in the Middle East, the Soviet Union has been the procurer of arms to the Arab states as the United States has been to Israel. In Asia, the United States has been fighting the war for South Vietnam, while North Vietnam has been receiving support from the Soviet Union and China.

The situations in Vietnam and the Middle East clearly illustrate the continued need of superpower agreement for any successful intercession by the United Nations in critical issues. The United States did not succeed in 1966 and 1967 in having Vietnam included in the agenda of the Security Council because of Soviet opposition. Evidently, the Soviet Union was above all concerned with its image of a sturdy advocate of North Vietnam's cause, which could be seriously hurt by negotiation and compromise. The Arab-Israeli war, too, shows the dependence of United Nations action on big power agreement. Hostilities could have been easily avoided by the Security Council. However, the Security Council was immobilized by the lack of Soviet cooperation. At the request of the Soviet Union the situation created by the war was brought before a special meeting of the General Assembly, rather than before the Security Council. Assembly action was frustrated by disagreement between the United States and the Soviet Union. The session was clearly dominated by the superpowers, and the members were divided into two contesting blocs. Although both sides presented resolutions moderating the initial positions of the superpowers, neither could devise a settlement acceptable to both.

The Middle East crisis permits a number of conclusions concerning the influence of the superpowers: the superpowers could have prevented open warfare, while their inaction encouraged open hostility; they were responsible for the cease-fire imposed upon the belligerents by the United Nations; they alone had it within their power to convert the local war into a major war or to prevent it from becoming one; they alone are capable of securing a stable peace settlement. The proceedings also reflect on the peacekeeping role of the United Nations. The divergence of the American and Soviet positions, which the debate revealed, turned the appeal to the United Nations into a stumbling block in the way of settlement. The hope for all-out United Nations support encouraged President Nasser to reject negotiations with Israel, thus precluding stabilization of relations through mutual recognition of rights and accommodation. Yet the rigid formula to restore the status quo on which he insists and which has been supported by the Soviet Union could only serve to perpetuate instability in the Middle East and provoke future wars.

Whether the United Nations will be able, in the future, to emancipate itself from its dependence on the big powers and become a force in its own right, is impossible to predict. For the foreseeable future, it may be expected that international politics will continue to be controlled by the superpowers whose competition provides the framework of contemporary world politics. It is within this framework that the United Nations and the lesser sovereignties must act.

CHAPTER SEVEN

IDEOLOGY, POWER, AND LAW

IDEOLOGY

The Stakes: Ideology or Power?

On the surface, the stakes of the bipolar conflict seem clear. Both contestants claim to be pursuing ideological goals from which it would be dishonorable and irresponsible to retreat. At the same time, each has condemned the opponent's ideological "fixations" or "aberrations" and has held out the promise of a happier world if the adversary could be made to relinquish his position. Soviet claims that the capitalist world and the communist world are inevitably headed for a showdown are well known. Americans have been no less self-righteous in proclaiming the universal validity and sanctity of their principles and in condemning the ideological position of Soviet leadership. On the basis of these convictions, Americans have been doubtful that the danger of war can recede as long as the current communist doctrine prevails in the Soviet Union.

There is nothing new or unusual in exalting ideology in either international or domestic politics. Ideological stress may, in fact, be considered the distinguishing mark of modern politics; it has dominated the political scene since the rise of modern mass democracy. The ideological clash has gained in intensity as a result of the universal truth claimed by the opposing camps. In fact, practical politics have been progressively adapted in this century to ideological universalism. International politics and international law have been detached from their European frame of reference and become worldwide in scope. In their endeavor to combine principles and political advantage, the Big Two have indulged in proclamations of universal ideals in the hope of enlisting all the peoples of the earth as friends and allies.

Ideological claims are suspect, not only because they bypass truth as an autonomous standard that is independent of action, but also because they lend themselves to the promotion of social action that is unrelated to truth and justice. Moreover, they tend to conceal political motivations. The Soviet Union furnishes a good illustration of this practice. Shortly after seizing power, the Soviet government began pursuing a *national* foreign policy similar to that of its predecessors, despite its contrary ideological commitments. This is not to say that ideology has not been a compelling force in Soviet politics. Soviet leaders do "think and act differently from the czars," and no accurate appraisal can ignore the momentum provided by their commitment to a way of life requiring a totalitarian political structure and single-party rule.[1] However, political action is usually based on a mixture of power and ideology; and a singular emphasis on ideology does not necessarily reflect actual priorities.

The basic motives beneath political contests are never easy to ascertain. In international relations with its singular emphasis on power, it is particularly difficult to determine whether power is amassed as an end in itself or as a means of attaining ideals. The relationship of means and ends is even less certain in the bipolar balance. An inordinately strong element of confusion is introduced by the contradiction between an overriding concern with power and the need for a universal ideology to prove the moral superiority of one's own cause over the opponent's. Yet the many boisterous and self-righteous proclamations of

the superpowers are often contradicted by an obvious reluctance to act in accordance with their professed convictions. This action is guided by completely practical reasons. Although the tendency of a divided world to view
the conflict in terms of good and evil precludes both mutual toleration and the conversion of the opponent, a crusade to extinguish the evil, of dubious wisdom under any
conditions, would be disastrous today. Since neither side
can afford such an extravagancy, policy becomes more
oriented toward improving one's power position vis-à-vis
the opponent.

There is no dearth of evidence to show the secondary
importance of ideological motivations, although the contestants have not always been clear on this point and have
more often been less than candid in their public pronouncements. The United States, generally prone to thinking in
terms of black and white, has tended to view itself in a
heroic light. Such a vision is appealing; but this self-delusion has been bought at the price of political rigidity and
ineptitude. The Soviet Union has been able to buy its
dreams cut-rate, largely because its ideology is more in
tune with present political realities than is American political thinking. Nevertheless, Soviet policy is a mixture of
ideology and power. The present formula of live and let
live combined with competitive coexistence effectively em-
braces both aspects. To be sure, Soviet pragmatism is not
new. Both the world revolution and the doctrine of inevitable military clash with the capitalistic world, as postulated
by orthodox Marxism, have long been compromised. It is
not unusual, then, that Soviet policy should have become increasingly pragmatic under the pressure of bipolar politics.

The experiences of the Soviet bloc have done little to
encourage ideological policies. Ideology has been found
wanting as a unifying force, as the lack of harmony within
the Soviet camp indicates. It is fully apparent by now that
Marxism is anything but a single global movement and
that not all communist powers have the same, or even
similar, aims. The Sino-Soviet break has been the greatest
single factor in undermining the myth of communist unity.
The lines of communication have been further attenuated

by the Chinese racial appeal, made at the Asian-African solidarity conference of February 1963, that sought to exclude the Soviet Union as a white European nation,[2] an attitude that is alien to Marxist dogma. Whatever ideological considerations are involved, the rift can easily be attributed to a growing divergence of interests. Surely, Soviet foreign policy is far less ideological today than is Chinese foreign policy.

Geography and national-racial considerations play a surprisingly important role in the communist camp. If an alliance continues to exist between the Soviet Union and China it exists for power-political purposes only. Undoubtedly, it is for practical, not ideological, reasons that China has repeatedly adopted a more conciliatory tone vis-à-vis the Soviet Union and stressed the need for Sino-Soviet unity, provided that the fundamental principles of Marxism-Leninism are adhered to and the method of "consultation on the basis of equality" is adopted.[3] There is good reason to suspect that the Chinese ambition is to lead the nationalist, anti-imperialist revolutionary process in the underdeveloped and nonwhite areas of the world. Therefore, any ideological factors that may be involved in the Sino-Soviet dispute are of the nationalist variety rather than Marxian. Difficulties have also developed in Eastern Europe, reflecting an economic and political nationalism too strong to succumb to the idyllic image of contentment in the Marxian family.

American policy is similarly practical in its basic orientation. The heterogeneity of the American alliance system is certainly difficult to explain in terms of the ideological protestations of the United States government. Ideology has not precluded close cooperation with such incompatible governments as those of Turkey, Portugal, and Spain. In seeking support of the newly emerged nations, the United States does not discriminate against those favoring communism or neutralism. The policy toward Vietnam illustrates the American pragmatism. It was not because of the denial of religious freedom that the United States ceased to support the Diem regime in South Vietnam but, rather, because it feared that the unpopularity of that government rendered it ineffective in the fight against the communists. Nor has the United States hesitated to develop a friendship with communist Yugoslavia. In the Western hemisphere too, the United States has not always insisted on ideological uniformity. It has not let its prejudices hinder amicable relations with dictatorial regimes in Latin America, nor has it consistently denounced them as unfit for inter-American cooperation. The ostracism of Cuba was in response to Castro's overconfidence, rather than based on a firm ideological commitment. The ideological diversity within the American-led bloc, in fact, is so great as to preclude a common designation.

If one takes the trouble to separate the actual policies of the two camps from the propagandistic pronouncements, the clash between communism and capitalism appears less formidable than the race for global supremacy between the United States and the Soviet Union. Instead of clearly drawn ideological fronts, there is a criss-cross of secular religions: nationalism opposing nationalism, racism facing racism, the demand for freedom of the small powers against the need to dominate of the big powers. Invariably, power considerations predominate in the end. The American inclination to dismiss communism as being without a moral basis and the Marxian conviction that a showdown between capitalism and communism is inescapable have not prevented an agreement on some form of coexistence. In fact, with the passage of time, both sides have become increasingly serious about the need for mutual adjustment.

The fury over ideological pronouncements has not prevented the mutual adaptation of the two blocs that is taking place despite vast differences in thought, political structure, and practices. Collectivism is growing in the United States at the same time that individualism is gaining, however modestly, in the Soviet Union. Observers have even spoken of the possibility of the Soviet Union and the United States joining forces if and when China emerges as a first-rate power. Although prognostications of this kind may seem far-fetched, they cannot be discounted on ideological grounds. It is perhaps plausible that the political development of the two blocs should converge, since in a bipolar

world both must face and meet similar problems in the
areas of industrialization, democratic development, and
preparation for and avoidance of total war.

In the light of such political developments, the American government has finally begun to view its foreign policy
from a less ideological perspective. President Kennedy
clearly deprecated the importance of ideology when he
stressed, in an address at The American University on June
10, 1963, the common interest of the United States and
the Soviet Union in preserving the peace and halting the
arms race. This attitude recurred in President Johnson's
appeal to the Soviet Union in August 1966 to "abandon
the dogmas and vocabularies of the cold war" and join the
United States in "rational acts of common endeavor." No
one can take such a position without being prepared to
abandon self-righteous aloofness in favor of direct communication and negotiation with a view to stabilizing the
present precarious nonbelligerency. The foremost interests
of both powers include prevention of nuclear diffusion and
securing control over their allies. This accounts for Soviet
efforts to restrain China from provoking war. The United
States has also met its obligations in this respect. Overcom-
ing its ideological propensities, it has not permitted the
rise of a revanchist German policy in the East, had accepted the good faith of the cryptocommunist government
of Sukarno before the 1965 *coup* as a basis for peace in
the Far East, and has sought friendly relations with the
Kadar government in Hungary.[4] Most important, it has
dropped all pretenses of trying to liberate Eastern Europe
from communist rule.

The Role of Ideology

It is a curious paradox that in an age when ideologies can
make ordinary people move mountains, ideological motives
are relegated to a secondary role in the international struggle. Their reduced importance, however, should not blind
us to the influence that ideologies continue to have even
today. It is certainly unrealistic to brush them aside as

mere rationalizations, invoked to obscure the brutality of the naked power struggle. The twentieth century has, with good reason, been termed an age of ideological politics and ideological wars. Secular religions have dominated its politics. Therefore, it should not be surprising that opposite ways of life and conflicting ideologies have aggravated the power struggle and have provided its rationale. The force of ideological aspirations has not been destroyed by the pragmatic nature of the present contest. In fact, the desire to protect one's independence and security and to ensure cultural identity and a way of life in accordance with a presumed standard of truth remains a formidable driving force.

The impact of such aims does not necessarily imply the need to eliminate other ways of life and ideologies. Nor can any thought of universal expurgation require serious consideration in a bipolar, nuclear world. Nevertheless, it is entirely possible that ideological factors may cloud the views of statesmen and cause them to blunder into disaster. Bipolar politics are highly susceptible to ideological influences and in turn tend to aggravate ideological cleavages. The dichotomy of global power is sufficient temptation to view the conflict in moral terms. This view is reinforced by the political fact that each side is possessed by both a pathological fear of the other's power and by its own universalist ideological pretensions. The fear is exacerbated by the dimensions of the conflict, the likelihood of political extinction by the victorious enemy, and the absence of shared moral values. There is little wonder, then, that the power issues of national security and survival are both obscured and compounded by the moral, ideological, and social clash, which, though a secondary motivation, is in the foreground of public attention.

Despite its secondary position as a motivating force, the effect of the ideological clash upon international politics is considerable. A world divided along ideological lines is not likely to be distinguished by moderation, a virtue that characterized the traditional balance of power politics. The finesse of the chess player has been displaced by the fe-

rocity of the piqued bull. A further inherent danger in
ideological thinking is the potentially calamitous tendency
to obfuscate issues. Erroneous judgments by Soviet leadership have provoked numerous crises since the end of the
Second World War. The repeated resuscitations of the explosive issues of Berlin, Korea, Quemoy and Matsu, the
Congo, and Cuba have reflected the Soviet lack of understanding of American temperament and thought, caused
largely by ideological preconceptions. Matters have been
made worse by linguistic confusion, which has normally
followed in the wake of ideological schisms. Different
meanings attached to identical terms have made communication between East and West extraordinarily difficult.
Although misunderstandings have often been manufactured
to confuse issues and gain political advantage, they, no
doubt, have been genuine at times and could have had
disastrous consequences at a critical moment.

Perhaps the most dangerous implication of the ideological approach to politics is the tendency to treat practical
wisdom as if it were dogma. This tendency, especially
marked in the bipolar world, can normally be expected
to produce not only international political divisions but also
corresponding internal disunity, since both sides claim to
possess the key to the salvation of mankind. Despite the
presence of such divisive forces, the United States and the
Soviet Union, as well as their major allies, are enjoying a
remarkable degree of internal unity. Divisions have only
occurred among some of the allies who, in the case of the
West, have been beset by serious social and economic dis-
ruptions or, in the case of the East, have been challenged
beyond the limits of endurance by nationalist sensibilities.
The extraordinary internal consensus can probably be explained by the strong appeal of nationalism—a force
greater than either communism or capitalist democracy.

Ideology has not only played a negative role in the bipolar struggle by confusing political thinking; it has also
played a positive role as a political tool, thereby acquiring
a position that would have been unlikely in the traditional
balance of power system. Inasmuch as the struggle for

power has largely been a struggle for control of the minds of men, ideology has become a weapon of primary importance. Contemporary public opinion has been averse to considering issues involving the possibility of universal annihilation in terms of pure, simple power. Therefore, it is not surprising that both sides have deemed it prudent to hold out the promise of creating an ideal world—be it by emancipating the proletariat through universal sovietization or by delivering the world from the evil of communism.

Although leaders of both sides may be aware of the paramountcy of political considerations, their peoples clearly are not, and they respond enthusiastically to ideological appeals. The Truman Doctrine, proclaimed by the President in 1947, illustrates this point. The President could not afford to act in defense of the power interests of the United States; an ideological justification—the Truman Doctrine—was required to assure the American people that its government was not acting in the manner of cynical "power politicians," but that it was embarking on a crusade to contain communism in all corners of the globe. In this way, the President could strengthen the moral position of the United States in the world, while satisfying the aspirations of his people for moral perfection in a Pax Americana. Despite the far-reaching effects of ideological attacks, the importance of ideology in the bipolar world is not in motivating the actions of statesmen but in its efficacy as a weapon.

The Paradox of Constitutional Conformity

It is understandable that in a divided world the primacy of power interests has not been able to shake the contestants' faith in the superiority of their own system. What is more difficult to comprehend is their conviction that peace and security depend on the existence of similar forms of government in other leading countries. Although the superpowers have frequently disregarded ideological consistency in favor of practical politics, a strong preference for similarly constituted systems is unmistakable. It would seem that, except when dictated by expediency, the governmental systems of other countries would be a matter of indifference. However, there is a psychological factor to be considered: Similar systems have a natural attraction for each other, and it would be idle to deny that shared values tend to create a sturdy bond between a hegemonial power and its satellites.

Nevertheless, strategic problems and embarrassments have arisen between similarly oriented governments; and on closer inspection it seems questionable that constitutional similarity is necessarily a strategic asset. A case can perhaps be made for the rationality of such a policy for the Soviet Union. Through ideologic control of communist parties outside the Soviet Union, Soviet leaders have often been able to direct the foreign policies of countries having communist governments. Yet even under such conditions, experiences have weakened this natural bond. Adherence to a common ideology and institutional similarity have not prevented resistance to direction from Moscow by such communist states as Yugoslavia, Albania, China, and more recently Rumania. It can, in fact, be said that the chief instrument of postwar Soviet imperialism has not been communism as much as technical and industrial power. But even if ideological control is not always dependable, it has often proved useful in drawing the newly rising nations into the Soviet camp, especially when ideology has joined forces with nationalism.

The strategic rationale of constitutional conformity is more difficult to see in the case of the United States. In contrast to communist dictatorships, democracies cannot be easily controlled. While dictatorial countries can be controlled through dictators, in democracies basic decisions are frequently made by the people or their representatives, who cannot be depended upon to yield to pressure by the hegemonial power.[5] However, the United States has not mechanically encouraged democratic or constitutional governments. In his address at The American University, President Kennedy declared that "we are unwilling to impose our system on any unwilling people," and charged the Soviet Union with a lack of respect for the right of political self-determination. However, it is often hard to determine when a people is willing to adapt itself to the political preference of the hegemonial power; therefore, a charge of interference is difficult to substantiate. There may also be some doubt that the tolerance expressed by the President is firmly supported by American thinking. The report of the Clay Committee, which, apparently, was favorably received in Administration circles, rejected the principle of noninterference in the affairs of other nations and strongly urged that very definite strings be attached to American economic aid. Nor has American diplomatic practice been unexceptionally adverse to interfering in the affairs of other nations. For example, the German constitution of 1949 was drafted upon orders of the Western occupational powers in accordance with rather specific instructions expressing their political preferences. Since then, the American government has repeatedly tried to influence elections in Germany and Italy, and even in more remote parts of the globe to ensure the survival of constitutional governments.

The practical interest beneath the ideological emphasis is nevertheless easy to detect. The election in 1963 of a leftist government in the state of Pernambuco, Brazil, created American concern that aid given under the Alliance for Progress to the new government might strengthen forces hostile to the United States.[6] Yet, different criteria applied to the American recognition of a military junta as the government of Korea—leadership that clearly does not meet American standards. One may conjecture whether the United States would have given its approval if the new Korean government had not proclaimed its fervent admiration for the United States.[7] Again, in 1964, the response to Cuban feelers for a possible reestablishment of Cuban-American relations was not made contingent upon a change in government but on its severing its "ties of dependency" on the Soviet Union and ceasing to promote subversion in Latin America.[8]

The foremost concern of the United States in bestowing

its favors then seems to be the willingness of governments to cooperate rather than to comply with American ideological preferences. The one major exception has been the refusal of the United States to recognize Communist China and to tolerate its admission into the United Nations. The American policy on China is not easily explained in terms of practical politics. But the ideologically motivated policy can be better understood if one recalls its genesis at a time when the cold war was new and the United States inexperienced. The persistence of that policy is probably due less to conviction than to necessity, since the United States has not been able to find a way of reversing it without losing face. The Soviet Union, though more inclined to remake other nations in its image, has also deviated from the general rule when expediency demanded it. A case in point is Soviet relations with the Arab countries. The wide gap between Moslem religiousness and communist atheism, ruling out conversion of Arab countries to communism, has not stood in the way of close diplomatic ties. Reportedly, the Soviet Union has given extensive military aid to noncommunist developing countries since the mid-1950's.[9]

If allowance is made for the primacy of practical considerations, there remain, nevertheless, sound political reasons for serious concern with the constitutional problem. The fusion and confusion of domestic and international politics, characteristic of the cold war, creates mutual sympathy among those of a similar political outlook and may, at times, form alliances even when national interests clash. For the United States, the decisive consideration often is the need to counter Soviet exploitation of constitutional conformity, regardless of the direct effect this may have on the susceptibility of others to its hegemonial influence. Frequently, the issue cannot be dodged, and neither side can afford to cease making extravagant claims for its system. The establishment of democracies may not have facilitated American control, but, in any event, it has been effective in undermining Soviet strategy. Experience has shown that the existence of a strong democratic government may render a country immune to Soviet influence.

POWER

Power and Morality

In addition to the role of ideology, it will be necessary to examine the impact of bipolarism upon the moral aspect of international relations. Perhaps no problem is more vital to a study of politics, and it is as relevant to international policy as to domestic relations, the chief difference being that in international relations, statesmen have less freedom in deciding whether to resolve their conflicts through violent or peaceful means. The frequent need to depart from peaceful diplomatic intercourse has long posed a moral predicament to responsible men. It has been a particular source of embarrassment to American statesmen, who have found it difficult to reconcile the demands of political reality with their faith in the possibility of moral action in both spheres. Their firm conviction that man is the master of his fate in international affairs as well as in other areas has strengthened their confidence that nations are always free to choose peace over war.

This exalted faith in the unrestricted possibility of moral action belies misconceptions of the nature of power. No attempt to cleanse power of injustice and brutality has ever succeeded. Nor has it been possible to eliminate power from human relations. But when appropriate reservations are made, power has a constructive role in establishing a measure of order in an imperfect world. It is naive to expect that order can exist totally free of injustice, or to assume, when a choice between order and justice cannot be avoided, that moral men can decide against order and still salvage justice. The sense of tragedy, never wholly lacking in international relations, has compelled contemporary American foreign policy to consider political necessity, as well as to employ the ruthless calculus of power, often in deference to the interests and obligations implied by its leading position.

The unsupported assumptions that state morality can be equated with individual morality and that concrete moral

principles of individual conduct are equally valid for nations has been a basic tenet of American political thinking.
Accordingly, it has influenced foreign policy. Social stability and a spiritual heritage have resulted in a tendency
to look upon moral rules as universally applicable, acceptable abstractions. Consequently, the close relationship of
rules of conduct to the social and political context, and
the need to limit moral choices to possible courses of action, have often received insufficient attention. Obviously,
neither individuals nor states are morally obliged to self-
destruction in the name of an abstract principle. In the
absence of clearly articulated international society and
effective international institutions, the right to survive confronts states, more dramatically than individuals, with the
moral dilemma of having to choose between greater and
lesser evils, denying them the range of choices that is available to individuals. The need to rely on self-protection often
requires action that would be reprehensible if committed
by individuals. A further complication of the moral problem arises from the possibility that general canons of morality may lead to ruin or surrender, so that defeatism
may, in the end, be less moral than determined, belligerent
action.

The absence of a necessary coincidence between political
prudence and specific moral norms is largely responsible
for the nebulousness of morality in international relations.
But even if collective survival should occasionally require
extreme action, there is no reason to exclude morality from
international relations by replacing the practical necessity
of power with an ideology of power. Actually, even the
most cynical of statesmen have rarely dismissed the moral
question as irrelevant, and they have gone to great lengths
to convince themselves and others of the righteousness of
their cause. There has never been a general acceptance of
arbitrary extensions of political necessity in justification of
monstrous acts. Civilized men have normally acknowledged
the dictates of reasonableness and humaneness as limits to
actions.

The question, then, is not whether sovereign collectivities are subject to a moral standard; few theoreticians and even fewer practitioners of statecraft have denied that they are. The values of the state are not supreme but must be fitted into the hierarchy of general human values. What remains problematical are the substantive moral principles applicable to states, since the absence of a suprastate government forces them to rely on their own devices for protection. For this reason, power in the relations among states can never be contained by fixed and universal moral maxims.

The cause of world order can be better served by conceding a dual standard of morality, distinguishing between canons applicable to individual men and sovereign collectivities, and not by insisting on universal principles incapable of national compliance. The absence of clear and unambiguous principles unfortunately harbors dangers that cannot be easily dismissed. In assuming the impossibility of formulating specific rules, one invites permissiveness and narrows the scope of morality. Legitimate questions may be raised that have no counterpart in individual morality. Is there an autonomous moral law in international relations? How much humaneness must be demanded in dealing with citizens of other states? Raising such questions often is the first step toward dismissing them as irrelevant. Too readily, morality is bent in favor of expediency and ideological interest is substituted for transcendental right. The tendency to nationalize universal principles is difficult to resist. Unless ways are found to make principles of state morality more specific, the danger of moral relativism looms large. Finally, in actual practice, the dual standard of morality may prove to be no standard at all.

Morality in the Bipolar World

If the need to define a specific standard of conduct for states in their mutual relations is clear, the difficulty of arriving at concrete principles remains. If statesmen cannot be expected to leave their societies exposed to the threat of annihilation, may they act in defiance of accepted standards of common sense and decency in the name of a vaguely defined or imaginary concept of public welfare? The major moral task facing statesmen is to translate general concepts of collective interest into specific rules of the type that civilized men can accept as a standard of action. The difficulty of the task should not be belittled. It is one thing to postulate that violence must remain proportionate to legitimate ends. But what is legitimate in international relations? And when is the point reached where the plight of a state justifies violent measures that would not be condoned under less desperate conditions?

The problem is further aggravated in a bipolar nuclear context. International morality has been rendered more tenuous than ever by the enormous stakes involved in the cold war, by the finality of a victory that may be won by either side, by the increased need for self-reliance resulting from the rigidity of the balance, the limited choices available, and the narrow scope of political maneuver. A number of questions come to mind which are in urgent need of answers. If any unused opportunity yields a double advantage to the opponent and only sustained aggressiveness can contain him, can bipolar issues ever be narrowed down so as to be susceptible to reasonable and mutually acceptable solution? If only aggressiveness can contain aggressiveness, what are legitimate ends in the cold war and how could nuclear warfare, if it were to occur, be limited?

Just action in the narrow sense is not always possible in international relations, even for moral men. Moreover, matters are not helped by the moral decay that has accompanied the progressively ideological orientation of politics. It could be argued that the policy of containment, which has been the United States' answer to bipolarism, is no more justifiable than Soviet expansionism, unless one is prepared to sanctify an unqualified status quo. But whatever moral objections might be raised against containment, it is difficult to find an alternative solution. The problem is not resolved by interposing the offices of the United Nations. Its decisions, too, are political in nature and bear no necessary relationship to morality or justice. United

Nations action cannot alter the fact that the rigidity of the bipolar balance has severely reduced the scope of available choices. And it remains as true in international relations as it does in personal relations that moral argumentation is irrelevant where no choices exist.

LAW

The problem of an international standard of conduct is even more acute in the realm of international law. While morality is concerned with general guiding principles and to a large extent remains subjective, law must provide specific and unambiguous rules. Its relationship to the social and political context in which it is to function is, therefore, even closer than that of morality. It may, consequently, be worth examining the continued appropriateness of traditional international law under the new distribution of power in a world of rapidly advancing armament technology. The many predicaments of American statesmen in recent years indicate that even the staunchest supporters of traditional law frequently find it impossible to act in accordance with its precepts without seriously endangering their country's security.

Bases and Aims of International Law

The status of international law has long been precarious and ambiguous and it is more frequently honored in its breaches than in its fulfillment. This does not, however, mean that its principles have no binding force. As one ascends the hierarchy of legal norms, the enforceability of rules becomes increasingly problematical, but this does not deprive them of their status as valid legal norms. This is as true of constitutional norms, which require legislative action to be enforceable, as it is of international law. The chief purpose of international law has been to enable the leading powers to maintain a measure of order in the world—admittedly on terms favorable to them. This has not been equivalent to the prevention or suppression of violence, and thus has a serious shortcoming. International lawyers have realistically confined themselves to regulating only that which is susceptible to regulation and have aimed to prevent violence from getting out of hand.

Stressing the pragmatic nature of international law does not lessen its normative character. Like all law, it not only rests on the shared values and purposes of the community, but also on a sense of right shared by civilized men. The highly pragmatic character of international law results from the limited consensus of international society; this limited consensus compares unfavorably with the sense of community present in domestic societies which rest, in turn, on a more stable institutional framework. The bases of consensus are especially weak in the contemporary international world. The extension to the entire globe of a legal system peculiarly Western European in origin and conception commanded less than universal admiration and respect. The overriding demands of political necessity in the bipolar world have been especially harmful to the efficacy of international law and make such endeavors as to "maintain peace through law" appear fatuous. More than ever peace has come to depend on a balance of destructive power.

Obsolescence of Traditional International Law

In recent years the plight of international law has been made increasingly obvious as American statesmen attempt to reconcile law with expediency. In spite of their professed commitment to international law, they have had to discover that the demands of American security frequently do not permit compliance with legal precepts. The abortive attempt to invade Cuba indirectly as well as the "quarantine" of the island are not easy to reconcile with the rules. Dilemmas of this nature have not, however, led to the reexamination of the adequacy of the law. Instead, a legal eclecticism has resulted, at the expense of formal consistency. It is impossible, for example, to reconcile the narrow legalism of the United States during the Suez crisis in 1956 and its pragmatic policy toward Cuba in 1962.[10] Rules of international law were equally strained in the famous U-2 affair, and difficulties of a similar nature might have arisen in the Congo had Lumumba lived and carried out his threat to invite the interposition of Soviet military forces.

The limited choices available today make it difficult to condemn breaches of the law if compliance with its rules would jeopardize survival or independence. There is little virtue in a legal order exacting observance to the point of self-destruction. It is common sense that any law, to be effective, must be adapted to the existing power structure. International law like municipal law is tied to a social and territorial order. Its binding force depends, in the final analysis, on its ability to stand the test of creating and maintaining order. Law, when reduced to an abstraction, not only loses its practical effectiveness, but also loses its moral basis; it requires a quality of choices made from existing practicable alternatives. In the light of the available choices, it may be impossible to condemn acts of questionable legality. One may be more inclined to question the adequacy of the existing law. This is not to deny the normative character of law but merely to stress the need for a reasonable relationship of the norm to man's actual social condition and moral nature.

Looking at traditional international law from the historical perspective, it is apparent that it was tailored to fit a world order that has now been displaced. Its outdated legal concepts have been a greater source of embarrassment to the United States than to the Soviet Union. Situations have arisen when compliance with the rules was strategically impractical, while noncompliance worked to undermine the American moral position. The major source of difficulty has been the self-delusion that there continues to be a close correlation between the present world order and the international legal system, designed, as it was, to regulate relations between mutually independent states that were fully responsible for their actions. However, incidents occur that do not permit a reconciliation of vital American interests with precepts derived from this imaginary order; and the United States has been no more willing than others to sacrifice its security to formal legality. Further, the Soviet Union has systematically exploited the American penchant for legalism and intervened in the affairs of other countries by making wars and revolutions by proxy.

THE PROBLEM OF THE THIRD DIMENSION   The inadequacies of international law fall into three major categories. One is related to the revolutionary technological innovations, while the other two pertain to the bipolarization of power. The first group can be disposed of briefly since it did not grow from political roots. Much confusion has existed since men began to utilize air space for military ends in the early part of the century. Unlike the law of the land and of the sea, an autonomous body of rules making up the law of the air has not thus far been developed. Rather, problems relating to air space have largely been dealt with by means of analogies derived from land and sea laws. The uncertainties of regulating the third dimension have been further aggravated by man's ventures into outer space and, by the revolution in armaments technology. Not only have nuclear missiles rendered obsolete the traditional means of delivering destructive devices to their targets and, therefore, stripped the pertinent legal rules of their content, but the effects of nuclear explosions can no longer be limited to specific targets. Consequently, the age-old attempt of international law to confine violence to more or less clearly defined areas and methods has proved futile. Even the modest successes of the past have been lost, and an entirely new approach to the problem of preventing universal chaos must be found.

THE LAWS OF PEACE AND WAR   The other two inadequacies are directly related to the bipolarization of power. They refer to the problems created by the cold war and the decline of sovereignty. Traditional law made a clear distinction between war and peace as legal conditions and provided separate sets of norms for each. That distinction is no longer appropriate to the cold war. In the absence of a technical state of war, present international relations are clearly guided by the laws of peace. Yet there seems to be small chance that the law of peace can actually cope with present conditions. Legally there is peace; but both sides think and act as if there were war. For the first time, the United States has imposed capital punishment for espionage in time of peace. It would, therefore, seem more realistic to acknowledge the present state of affairs as a condition that is neither peace nor war, but a new development in international relations.

International law should be more closely adapted to the facts of international life by the creation of the legal state of "cold war" to govern the international relations of the superpowers. Such a state would be better attuned to the contemporary condition than the traditional law, with its two-fold division between laws of peace and laws of war. A leading authority, P. C. Jessup, has thoughtfully suggested the creation of a third state of "intermediacy." [11] But the cold war is not an intermediate condition. Moreover, the proposal leaves unsolved the practical problem of invoking the state of intermediacy. Much confusion would be removed and peace would rest on a more secure foundation if the unique position of the Big Two in international politics were reflected in a special status under international law. The "cold war" law would supersede the traditional laws of peace by acknowledging in its rules the de facto precedence of the strategic needs of superpowers. It would be little concerned with the rules of warfare, which are rendered useless by the fact that nuclear war between the major powers cannot be limited. Despite the ample concessions traditionally made to the ulterior demands of war, there remains little place for a law designed to reduce permissiveness in war. The law of "cold war" would therefore be oriented more toward political and economic matters than military ones.

It could be argued that the abolition of the laws of peace and war in superpower relations would represent retrogression inasmuch as the traditional definitions of legal rights and duties imposed some limitations, however rudimentary, on international relations in both peace and war. But in actual fact, it is doubtful that much of anything would be surrendered by making such a change. It is worth recalling that during the two world wars of the twentieth century the limitations of warfare already suffered serious setbacks.

They have become completely pointless in relation to contemporary armaments and under the political exigencies of bipolar war, neither of which is susceptible to restraints. It seems reasonable to assume that between the superpowers the threat of a military war has disappeared, except as an apocalyptic spectacle, since it has ceased to be a rational means of executing policy. If it comes, it is likely to signal the end of civilization and perhaps of all life. The present rules of law designed to limit the radius and effect of destructive force become inapplicable where total destruction is an attainable end. They retain, at most, some usefulness in brush-fire actions.

THE WANING OF SOVEREIGNTY   The final inadequacy of traditional international law in the bipolar age is that the entire system is based on the theory of sovereignty. International legal theory, as formulated by Hugo Grotius in the seventeenth century, accepts the sovereign state as the basic and ultimate unit of international society, coexisting with a sizable number of other mutually independent and approximately equal states. Such categories fit the political facts of a limited period of history (1648–1945), but are of little pertinence in the bipolar world, where most sovereignties have declined while two have risen to clear dominance. Neither the superpowers nor the lesser sovereignties fall into these catagories any longer.

The decline of the sovereign state casts serious doubt not only on the obligatory force of specific norms but also on the suitability of the traditional system as a universally binding legal order. Its inability to distinguish between the different types of units that are subject to it has removed it so far from political reality as to impair both its practical and moral force. If it is the peculiar responsibility of the two superpowers to maintain world order, and if their special status and rights are legally acknowledged, they are sharply set off from the rest of the nations. This implies the rejection of universal state equality, thereby questioning the validity of the legal order that is based on the premise. If we continue, nonetheless, to speak and think in terms of equal and universally valid rules, we must expect to encounter problems that are insolvable in legal terms.

The Dilemma of Intervention The rules of traditional international law have been challenged—in deeds rather than in words—by both leading powers, not out of contempt, but because of the practical impossibility of compliance. The dilemma is most strikingly illustrated by the subject of intervention. There has always been the temptation for the strongest states to ignore the injunctions against intervention in the internal affairs of other states. The problem has, however, become more serious in the bipolar age, when intervention has ceased to be the mere expression of the *élan vital* of vigorous and powerful nations and has become a strategic necessity even for those who would prefer to remain within legal bounds.

The present tendency for international war to assume the guise of civil war does not permit indifference toward internal developments in strategically important areas. The result has been that international law is frequently bypassed. The fusion of international and civil war has enabled the superpowers to evade its formal injunctions by applying coercion through diplomatic, political, or economic pressures that lie beyond the scope of its authority. Yet it cannot be denied that such pressure can be a singularly effective means of intervention. Although a country is theoretically free to accept or decline aid that is offered, the unsatisfactory level of its development frequently leaves it little actual choice; once it has accepted, it has exposed itself to outside influence. The line between pressure and persuasion is therefore not easy to draw. Military bases raise similar problems. Under traditional law, the construction of bases is unobjectionable if the government of the host country agrees. But to obtain such agreement, it may be first necessary to change the government or perhaps even the political system. This can often be done indirectly by promoting revolutionary activity through propaganda and the dispatch of trained "volunteers."

De facto interference may thus bypass the defenses of the sovereign state. The effects may be so far-reaching that nothing less than direct intervention can undo them. This accounts for the vacillations of the superpowers in relation to such action. Inconsistencies in interpreting the law should not, perhaps, cause any great surprise in the case of the Soviet Union, since in Marxian thought, law has no intrinsic value and is easily made to fit political expediency. However, the vacillations of American policy merit more serious attention. In theory, the United States has frowned on interventions of any kind. In Latin America, it has unconditionally renounced its own right to intervene in domestic affairs. It has tried to hold the Soviet Union to the same standard. In 1948, the United States government issued a stern warning to the Soviet Government not to intervene in Yugoslavia when that country defected, with American support, from the Soviet bloc. Here, the United States left little doubt that it would consider Soviet military intervention a sufficiently serious breach of international law to warrant belligerent countermeasures. In the Suez episode of 1955–1956, the United States refused to tolerate Anglo-French intervention despite the legal justification of such action in terms of broken treaty obligations by the Egyptian government. The obligations of Great Britain and France to seek redress via the United Nations were problematical in view of the Security Council's inability to act. Certainly, the United States, having bypassed the United Nations more than once for that very reason, was hardly in a strong position to uphold the United Nations as the only legal source of a solution.

Interestingly enough, American views have been less legalistic when intervention seemed necessary for the protection of its own vital interests. For example, the United States warned Italian voters in the early 1950's that American help would be withdrawn if the elections reflected a lack of support for the West. More seriously, in the follow-up of the interposition in Greece in 1947 great liberties were taken by the military and technical missions in directing the internal policies of the country. More recently the United States encouraged a military *coup* in South Vietnam. The most striking incident, however, was the economic retaliation and military use of Cuban refugees in attempts to dislodge the revolutionary government of Fidel Castro. The rupture of relations and the Bay of Pigs invasion—occurring before the construction of Soviet missile bases—cannot be reconciled with international law by invoking the doctrine of self-defense. It would require uncommon ingenuity to show that the United States, with its unrivaled defense system, was so seriously threatened as to be exceptable from the general prohibitions of international law. Cuba's right of self-defense against American hostilities and its legal freedom to invite the help of its Soviet ally similarly carries no less weight than the United States' right of self-defense, under a legal system designed to regulate relations between sovereign equals.

The United States has found it difficult to live up to its agreement to neutralize Laos, and has alternately pressured and baited internal forces in ways that closely resemble intervention. Moreover, the United States has increasingly resorted to military intervention. The intervention in Vietnam certainly has questionable legality. The massive involvement of American military forces in the Dominican Republic, and the occupation of its capital in the spring of 1965, furnishes a clear example of outright military intervention. Compelling political arguments can be made to justify such actions, but they are difficult to reconcile with existing international law.

Soviet policy has not been very different in this respect. The Soviet Union has intervened to protect its vital interests, and has tolerated American interventions if they could not be counteracted without the danger of provoking a major war. This, evidently, was the case in Greece, Laos, and Cuba.

These examples may suffice to suggest that the main carriers of the present order are required for reasons of political survival, to take action that cannot be reconciled with the existing rules of law. The defense of bloc solidarity by the hegemonial power may technically be intervention while de facto interference in the opponent's bloc may be perfectly legal. From the political point of view, the United States actually had a better case in Cuba than in Yugoslavia, and the Soviet actions in Hungary and East Germany, as well as its threats against Yugoslavia, have greater merit than the attempt to gain a foothold in the Western Hemisphere by strengthening Cuba militarily. Yet the reverse is true from the legal point of view. American measures to eliminate the Soviet foothold in the neighboring island were infractions of international law on more than one score, whereas the support of Yugoslavia was nothing more than a legally permissible interposition at the request of the established government.

Under circumstances such as these, international law leads to political absurdities. In the bipolar world, intervention may well be a necessity if bloc unity is to be maintained. The sensitivity of the superpowers to any interference by the opponent within their sphere of influence is understandable. The American build-up of Yugoslavia was as little acceptable to the Soviet Union as the presence of a communist government and missile bases in Cuba is to the United States. An international law that is impotent in the face of such situations will do more to disrupt than to stabilize world peace.

Collectivism   The United States has tried to extricate itself from the predicament by searching for ways of legalizing interventions that it considers vital to its security. The most promising approach appears to be collective action. This would make possible the protection of a sphere of influence through intervention by defense pacts or by regional organizations. The containment of Soviet expansion into uncommitted areas through collective United Nations action is an example. The case of Cuba is instructive; the United States tried to eliminate the problem without direct unilateral intervention by invoking collective action of the Organization of American States. In this way, intervention was quasi-legal and could be undertaken without adverse political effects. American efforts have not always produced political results. The only results of the OAS meeting held at Punta del Este in January 1962 were the application of rather mild political sanctions and the imposition of an arms embargo against Cuba. The reasons for the organization's failure to take more effective action as requested by the United States were partly legal and partly political. Legally there was no basis for intervention in the absence of a threat to the territorial integrity or the political existence of

Cuba. Politically the organization is committed to the two frequently contradictory principles of nonintervention and support of representative democratic systems. Whenever these principles have clashed, the Latin Americans have chosen nonintervention, and can be expected to do so in the future. In essence, they are motivated by the fear that even in a worthwhile case, the intentions of the United States may not be wholly honorable, and that collective action may set a precedent for future North American interventions in Latin America. Consequently, the deliberations of the inter-American organization tend to be cast in terms of a curiously accentuated legalism that is at odds with the predominantly political orientation of contemporary world politics. The evident rationale is the Latin American states' concern for their independence, as favored by traditional law. It is therefore not surprising that they were unwilling to sanction collective military intervention in Cuba even for the purpose of eliminating the Soviet foothold in the Hemisphere. Only when the communist threat became more concrete during the missile crisis and by Cuban aggression against Venezuela was the organization ready to take more definite action.

At the bottom of these difficulties lies the discrepancy between the theoretical assumptions of the international legal system based on the sovereign state, and the de facto decline of state power as a result of technological and political developments. Nonintervention was a workable doctrine only as long as sovereignty was a political fact. Now that sovereignty has been reduced to a status without material foundation, nations no longer have a convincing claim to the inviolability of territory they cannot defend. The disparity between legal and political status has not been appreciably diminished by the growing demands for equality of rapidly multiplying lesser sovereignties. Many of the problems that appear insolvable today may perhaps be eliminated through a greater concordance between law and fact. In the Cuban case, territorial sovereignty has stood in the way of a reduction of tensions either through unilateral or collective action. If such tensions persist, law alone is not likely to deter American intervention. It is more likely that international law, if it remains unrevised, will be sacrificed for political necessity.

The Need for Revision

To suggest that international law is in need of a fundamental revision is not to plead for its abolition. Despite the attitude of the "realists," it is an error to think that international law can be discarded altogether. History shows that a state of total lawlessness has never endured among individuals or organized groups of men. There have been times, however, when basic changes in political relations have demanded drastic modifications of the legal order. This was the case in the seventeenth century when Hugo Grotius deemed it necessary to adapt the basic principles of law to the new political fact of the sovereign state. The reason for the new law was eminently practical and fully vindicated by its pragmatic success.

A similar basis for revision exists today: The sovereign state has declined politically. The persistent belief in a one-world universalism that considers all states as more or less equal in rights and obligations and as subject to the same law is based on an illusion. It will not do to accept a legal universalism a priori, and to try to reshape the world to fit that abstraction. Unfortunately, statesmen are often oblivious to the limits imposed upon human action by historical developments. A good illustration is furnished in the opening speech of Adlai Stevenson before the United Nations General Assembly in September 1962 in which he said, "it remains to the Assembly to manifest its respect by converting the law into policy." [12] This thinking reverses the more normal process by which practice is crystallized into law.

Such a substitution of the exception for the rule may have unfortunate consequences. It has been associated with a prevalent American commitment to the quest for a one-world law and a one-world organization. This quest, pursued with varying intensity, has had serious repercussions in American diplomacy. The policies have not only been disparaged by communists. The late Secretary-General, Dag Hammarskjold, a dedicated civil servant of the United Nations, implicitly rejected such notions, pointing out that a balance had to be struck between the rights and obligations of the big powers and those of all the other nations.[13]

The clash between law and the dictates of politics has stimulated attempts by legal scholars to develop new approaches. They have generally preferred the cautious procedure of adapting the rules of traditional law to new situations to a vigorous reexamination of the basic premises on which the law rests. The more daring projects have moved in the direction of developing world law within the institutional framework of a world organization. Such projects, however, are little more than attempts to carry the traditional universalism of international law to its logical conclusion. But the problem of changing the law is not one that can be solved through judicial adaptation. It is a problem to be solved on the political plane by the big powers. The great contributions made by small nations should not obscure the fact that it has always been the great powers that have set the tone and provided the content of international law. In the nineteenth century that was the task of Great Britain. Today it belongs to the United States and the Soviet Union, who share the responsibility for, and have the greatest interest in, maintaining order.

The preparation of draft codes of peaceful coexistence has received growing attention in recent years, most recently at the Conference of the International Law Association in Brussels in August 1962.[14] Although at the Tokyo meeting in August 1964, the project was abandoned in favor of the more modest search for "principles of international security and cooperation," [15] the proceedings are of interest as an illustration of the difficulties caused by the competition and mutual distrust of the superpowers.

It is one thing to acknowledge the need for adapting international law to new international relations, but the obtrusiveness of the cold war remains a disturbing element. The very drive for codification can easily be perverted into a propaganda weapon. The United States, oriented as it is toward protecting the status quo, is fearful that the needed revision may subvert its position in ways that cannot be foreseen. Political circumstances, nevertheless, force it to keep the discussion going, since refusal to do so would leave it open to the charge of war-mongering.

Similarly, the contributions of the Soviet Union have belied its professed enthusiasm. Anxious to preserve its freedom to maneuver, its proposals have been so vague as to be meaningless. The chief purpose of the Soviets has been to extend their influence as far as possible by winning the sympathy of the neutralist bloc. At the same time, the Soviet Union has not been unmindful of the opportunities provided by traditional international law. Hence, it has made many proposals along orthodox lines while it is actively utilizing the subtle methods of the cold war, against which traditional international law provides no defense. By circumventing territorial sovereignty, the Soviet Union has been able to reconcile efforts to revolutionize world affairs with its role as standard bearer of those doctrines of traditional law that are held in high esteem by the new nations. Proposals emphasizing national self-determination, territorial integrity, sovereign equality, nonintervention, anticolonialism, disarmament, and cooperation cannot fail to appeal to colonials who are clamoring for independence; they may even generate support among the neutralist and pacifist liberals within the American bloc.

While it is true that national self-determination and anticolonialism are not standard doctrines of international law, they have for some time been in the mainstream of Western international thinking. From the Soviet point of view, these doctrines have the virtue of bypassing the Soviet strategy of ideological penetration and conquest through civil war. By contrast, American proposals have been more revolutionary in appearance. Although the United States has insisted on such orthodox features as respect for treaty obligations and the peaceful settlement of disputes, it has moved in new directions by advocating the inclusion of provisions for free cultural exchange without censorship (unless designed to produce civil strife), preparations of colonies for self-government, economic aid, the prohibition of military aid, and complete disarmament with effective controls. But on closer inspection, these departures seem less inspired by a search for new law than by the hope that the existing order can be salvaged through reforms accommodating the aspirations and claims of the rising colonial peoples, that would ensure a gradual transition.[16]

The differences in the methods of attacking the problem are not too serious and do not seem to preclude the possibility of compromises. However, the fundamental political disagreements of the superpowers stand out clearly in the interpretation of mutually accepted norms. Both the United States and the Soviet Union have given full support to the sanctity of treaty norms. But, while the United States is committed to an equal respect for all treaties, the Soviet Union proposes to accord top priority to the norms created by bilateral treaties and would deny obligatory force to "unequal treaties," that is, treaties between "imperialist" and dependent nations.[17] The United States has found such discriminatory interpretations unacceptable and has tried to close the loopholes left by the vagueness of the Soviet proposals through agreement on specific rules. Such differences, as well as a fundamental disagreement on the bases of law, would indeed seem to deny obligatory force to international law were it not for a strong desire on both sides for accommodation. An interesting point has been made by the Soviet legal scholar, Professor G. I. Tunkin, who suggested that disagreement concerning the nature and norms of international law does not necessarily preclude agreement on specific rules.[18] There is, in fact, much to commend this view, as both powers have a common interest in avoiding open warfare, in seeing their authority respected within their respective blocs, and in a clearer definition of inter-bloc relations, especially with regard to permissible economic relations between the opposing bloc and their own satellites.

The possibility of mutual accommodation is comforting, but it must be noted that it leaves little room for the legal universalism that has characterized the development of international law in recent times. In actual practice the first step in the new direction has already been taken. As one stu-

dent has aptly remarked, the decline of neutrality is a
precondition of any universalist international law,[19] because it reflects the general attenuation of sovereignty. A
similar conclusion is implied in the practical need to differentiate between various types of powers and their status
in terms of the function they perform in international
society.

Essentials of Bipolar Law

It is not within the scope of this study to make specific
proposals for a concrete framework of a bipolar international law. Rather, some fundamental problems will be
discussed and the general nature of the required legal
changes will be indicated. First, the political basis of bipolar
as well as traditional law is the right of self-preservation
and the need to rely on self-defense. However, bipolar law
would have to concede a greater role to self-reliance and
substitute hegemonial blocs for the national state as the
basic international unit.

The defense of the respective blocs would imply, on the
one hand, the need to concede to the hegemonial powers the
right to prevent outside intervention and, on the other, to
maintain sufficient cohesion within to render the bloc an
effective defensive unit. Bipolar international law would
therefore have to substitute, for the equal and universally
applicable rules of traditional law, separate and distinct
bodies of rules governing different types of relations. Four
different categories of international relations can be usefully
distinguished in the bipolar world: (1) rules applying to
relations between the two superpowers; (2) rules governing intrabloc relations between the superpower and its
satellites; (3) transbloc relations between and with opposing
satellites; and (4) rules applying to relations between and
with neutrals.

A change in the structure of the international legal system along these lines would not be as radical an innovation
as it might seem. An early step in this direction was taken
by the United States when it formulated the Monroe Doctrine as a principle of its foreign policy.[20] In claiming a

special interest in and a special relationship with the geographic space of the Western Hemisphere, at the expense of the sovereign rights of the states within the area as well as of extra-American powers, it, in fact, rejected the universalism that was taking shape elsewhere in the Western world. The incompatibility of the Monroe Doctrine with universalist principles is reflected by the European powers' rejection of it as a doctrine of international law. But if the Monroe Doctrine was of dubious validity in the past, the spatial principle on which it rests is peculiarly up to date in the bipolar world. This is not to say that it can apply today in every detail. Its uniqueness as well as its geographic restriction is clearly outdated. The worldwide commitments of the United States require the extension of a special relationship to the entire bloc for which the United States claims leadership.

The same reasoning applies to the Soviet bloc, and it is necessary to acknowledge as legitimate a similar doctrine for its sphere. If all-out war is to be avoided, the Soviet orbit must be accorded as much respect as the United States. This is not to suggest that it would be possible or desirable to stake out clearly circumscribed, stable spheres by means of formal agreement. It is not to be expected that the lines of the hegemonial blocs will be any more immutable than state boundaries were in the past, or that bipolar law will provide greater protection for them than traditional law provided for the territorial integrity of the sovereign state. But a change along the suggested lines would remove the legal obstacles presently in the way of preserving hegemonial control within the blocs the superpowers reasonably claim as their domain.

The acceptance by the Big Two of new relationships outside the scope of traditional international law actually has proceeded further than is generally recognized. Both powers have given evidence of a tacit agreement not to challenge the status quo to an extent that would lead them to the brink of war. They also seem to have recognized their mutual control and responsibility as bloc leaders.[21] For example, no serious attempt was made by the United States to intervene in East Berlin or Hungary during the uprisings.

Neither did Khrushchev appear overly convinced of the legitimacy of Soviet presence in Cuba, and he did not insist on a *quid pro quo* for the withdrawal of his forces and installations.[22]

The two powers have also made no secret of their common interest in establishing minimum rules to ensure the prevention of an unwanted nuclear war set off by lesser nations. They seem agreed that the ultimate decision to make war is their prerogative and have repeatedly proclaimed the desirability of preventing the diffusion of nuclear power.[23] And the limited nuclear test ban treaty, a first step toward establishing effective control, indicates their mutual effort. It is interesting to note that the United States has been firm in insisting that nations receiving atomic assistance for peaceful purposes submit to American or international inspection. The special status of the superpowers in this realm has been the subject of a recent Israeli complaint that international controls largely exempt the nuclear powers.[24] Thus far, such policies have been quite effective; only France and China are free from nuclear control.

The mutual desire for accommodation supports the inclination of Western jurists to avoid the hazards of codification and to proceed pragmatically, solving *ad hoc* problems as they arise. The method of effecting the change is, actually, of no great theoretical import. The relevant test is not in the genesis of the rules but in their effectiveness. However, there remains cause for uneasiness. The frequent intolerance of Soviet deviations from traditional norms is no sure indication that the United States appreciates the full extent of the change. The United States fails to acknowledge the parallels between its hegemony in the Western hemisphere and Soviet dominance in the East; it assumes its claims as a matter of course and, thus, is unable to see the need for a critical reappraisal of containment as a universal policy. Although the United States, by and large, has practiced admirable restraint in relation to the opponent's sphere, other hegemonial spheres have occasionally been invaded, particularly in Southeast Asia. The military involvement in Vietnam is a dramatic illustration of the

American determination to contain communism even in remote areas.

It must be cautioned, however, that it would be hazardous to ignore the dangers inherent in a "law of spheres"; it might permit the superpowers to emancipate themselves from restraints in dealing with lesser countries. A sense of unlimited power might also have disastrous consequences for the fundamental human rights of the subjects under the powers. Whenever large hegemonial systems emerge, there is cause for concern. The danger of lawlessness following the rejection of legal universalism was exemplified by the German occupation of Europe in the Second World War, and it is perhaps no accident that as far back as 1941 Carl Schmitt, the leading legal theorist of Nazi Germany, should have developed one of the earliest schemes of an international law based on spheres of influence or control.[25] The scheme evoked justified skepticism abroad as a transparent camouflage for Nazi designs at world domination.

The difference between the position of Nazi Germany and the situation now is that the decline of the sovereign state was not a political fact at that time and the multiplicity of leading powers had not as yet been reduced. Today the revolutionary redistribution of power is an obvious fact. The leadership of the United States and of the Soviet Union is neither the figment of anybody's imagination nor the result of a sinister scheme; it is the undeniable product of historical accident. Of all the fears evoked by this new state of affairs, none can cause more trepidation than the fate of human rights. Nothing can be said to alleviate such fears, but it should be pointed out that these rights have never been more in jeopardy than they are under traditional international law, inasmuch as the inviolability of state sovereignty prevented any interference with domestic matters. The record of bipolar law is not likely to be worse in this respect. It is, in fact, conceivable that a broadening of the right of intervention may prevent such monstrous atrocities as those Nazi Germany perpetrated for so long without fear of retribution.

CHAPTER EIGHT | CONCLUSION

Bipolarism has left its imprint on international relations since the end of the Second World War. Its effect has not been limited to relations between the two major powers and other states; bipolarization has also been accompanied by the rivalry and conflict of these two states, resulting in a cold war that is likely to persist as long as the international distribution of power remains bipolar. The extent of the changes this situation has caused is not always obvious. Established forms, having molded men's thinking for many centuries, do not yield easily, and the persistence of accustomed modes of thought in the face of new realities has often given rise to bewildering contradictions. The new conditions cannot, of course, be solely attributed to bipolarism; to a considerable extent, they must be credited to technological innovations. It is often difficult to relate specific changes in international relations to one phenomenon or the other. Generally, policy has been the result of the two closely connected phenomena: bipolarism and armaments technology. It is the technical superiority of the Big Two that has produced bipolarism, while bipolarism, in its turn, has given impetus to the technological race, responsible for the immense and rapid widening of the power gap between the two superpowers and third states.

Of the many paradoxes of bipolar international relations, the most fundamental is the attenuation of de facto sovereignty at a time when the number of sovereign states is sharply increasing, and even the smallest and least powerful are pursuing their sovereignty with unprecedented vigor. Although sovereignty is acquiring a new sanctity, it becomes increasingly apparent that the line between domestic and foreign politics has become blurred, and that the Big Two have become important political factors in the internal affairs of many countries through alliances, protection, diplomatic pressures, and economic and military aid. In reality, the nation-state has become obsolescent as an effective power unit. However, it has been shielded from obliteration by the resurgence of intense nationalism. The sentiments thus evoked have been sufficiently strong to block the transformation of the hegemonial alliances into genuine political units, in spite of the expanded sense of community within each camp. Moreover, cold war conditions have permitted third nations to act as an important restraining influence, often causing the Big Two to proceed more cautiously than they might otherwise. Regardless of their influence, third states have not been able to dissolve the great alliance systems, which have shown remarkable stability; nor have they succeeded in wresting from the superpowers the ultimate power of decision concerning the future of the world. The persistence of formal alliances may not appear to have great political significance in the light of existing substantive disagreements, which, on occasion, are expressed with considerable vehemence. Yet, continued membership and frequent support on major issues indicates that the overwhelming number of allies identify their vital interests with the overall policies of the hegemonial power.

The Big Two have increasingly come to apply—whether unconsciously or by design—a dual standard in measuring their actions and those of third powers. The gap that has arisen between the form and substance of international relations has created no formidable intellectual difficulties for the Soviet Union; contradictions are no problem to dialecticians. The divergence between theory and practice has been more problematical for the United States, which is torn between its theoretical commitment to universal canons of law and morality and the need to follow the exigencies of political realism. For example, the United States has unflinchingly insisted on retaining national control of its nuclear weapons while denying the same privilege to its allies. In relations with the Western Hemisphere, it has vigorously asserted its special status, while actively challenging China's right to claim a sphere of influence in southeast Asia. It has unilaterally assumed the task of maintaining world order on terms commensurate with its own particular preferences. The effort made by President Kennedy to give American foreign policy a broader basis by drawing the allies into a partnership has long since been put on ice by Washington.

The paradoxes of bipolar international politics are most noticeable in the relations between the United States and the Soviet Union. The possibility that tensions can be removed through a settlement of the basic issues is remote. Therefore, the military and political equilibrium remains precarious. But despite its vulnerability, the bipolar balance has shown a surprising stability and is likely to do so in the future. Again, it is paradoxical that the intense military competition of the superpowers occurs in a setting that makes the possibility of a military clash appear relatively remote. Clearly, weapons are forged less to perform their primary function than to serve the secondary purposes of keeping the cold war cold and implementing cold war strategy. In this type of warfare, armaments and military strategy are as much adjuncts of propaganda warfare as economic and ideological measures, and therefore are subordinated to the requirements of political strategy. A similar paradox is the discrepancy between the real and apparent ends of the struggle. The fierce ideological competition has all the appearances of a holy crusade. It is often forgotten, in the heat of the contest, that the basic issue is political, and the ideological crusade is largely a subsidiary tactical device.

The persistence of trouble spots and continued friction tends to conceal the happy fact that there has been a tacit mutual accommodation of the two superpowers. This is not to suggest that explicit agreements have been reached or that competition and vigilance are things of the past. However, the existence of a remarkable congruity between the basic interests of the two powers has become more apparent. Evidently, both are equally desirous to avoid all-out war. Both have demonstrated that they prefer continued bipolarism to a more diversified power structure and that they are particularly averse to the proliferation of nuclear weapons. Both have subordinated ideological interests to political ones. And, there seems to be essential agreement that the objective of the relentless arms race is a military stalemate, rather than war.

A potential source of confusion is the relative strategic importance of the various theaters of action. Overtly, attention has shifted to the peripheral areas. The focus of American policy, in particular, has shifted from the Atlantic area and Europe to the Pacific, and China has displaced the Soviet Union as the major object of American concern. But, here too, appearances are deceiving. Potentially, the most explosive areas continue to be the lands adjacent to the dividing line in Europe. It is not far-fetched to assume that, were either Western or communist forces to cross the Elbe River, full-fledged war between the two superpowers would become unavoidable. Although events in Asia or the Middle East may spark an all-out war, it is more probable that the war would originate in Europe. Changes in the peripheral areas, although important, can be far more easily tolerated than minute territorial shifts in Europe.

On the surface, these paradoxes might suggest that bipolar international relations are marked by a high measure of irrationality and uncertainty and, therefore, the likelihood of a major explosion has been enhanced immeasurably. However, this conclusion is not borne out by the facts. On the contrary, it can be demonstrated that present inter-

national politics have acquired an unusual degree of rationality. Notwithstanding disagreements and animosities, the
fear of nuclear war and its consequences have created a
universal sense of human fate. The growing awareness that
there can be total destruction following in the wake of a
nuclear war, has stabilized the relations between the superpowers to the extent that their diplomatic and political
moves are rationally calculated to a point unknown in the
annals of international relations. Thus, the danger that war
may start for flimsy or emotional reasons is more remote
than ever before. The relative contentment of the two leading powers with their position in the world leaves little
room for reckless maneuvers. Nevertheless, should open
war break out, it will be less the result of calculation than
of blunders, or possibly of uncontrollable tensions, that the
arms build-up may generate against all intentions.

It is impossible to anticipate, with any confidence, how
the balance of power of the future will shape up. Conceivably, effective power will once again be diffused. But
if this were to happen, a return to the traditional multiple
power pattern with its built-in, automatic checks against the
threat of world despotism would be highly unlikely. A
multipower system under present technological conditions
would be vastly different from anything known in the past.
Diffusion of nuclear weapons would mean one of two
things: Either a number of nations would possess the means
of inflicting total destruction upon the world and thus,
would be in a class with the United States and the Soviet
Union; or no other nation, even if equipped with nuclear
arms, would possess destructive capabilities to match those
of the United States and the Soviet Union. In either case,
traditional alliance policies of pooling military resources
would be obsolete. Under a multiplicity of first-rate nuclear
powers, no alliances would be needed to enhance the military power of any state, since there is nothing to be gained
from multiplying total destructive power. In the event that
a significant nuclear gap between the Big Two and the other
powers continues to exist, no pooling of resources would
be likely to produce a force capable of challenging the

superpowers. Certainly, neither contingency would provide the setting for a balancing power that could deter major upsets in the international balance of forces by throwing its weight in with the weaker side. When several countries have the means to destroy entire continents, it matters very little whether any weight is added to one side or the other.

Much will depend on the future relations between the United States and the Soviet Union. If they can find a basis for cooperation, they will be able to perpetuate the present distribution of power, which would be the most promising course for the future of the world. The present power structure would enable the Big Two to maintain order in the world on their terms. In particular, they could restrain the new nations from unreasonable and aggressive behavior. At the same time, the tensions that would necessarily persist between the superpowers would be a reasonable insurance against the reduction of other nations to peonage.

The existence of these conditions does not appear far-fetched. The most consequential development since the emergence of bipolarity has been the stabilization of the two opposing camps. Neither of the Big Two has made any major forays into the opponent's sphere. In fact, it seems safe to conclude that, as they have approached a nuclear stalemate, both major powers have increasingly identified with the status quo in international relations. It is noteworthy that China has openly accused the Soviet Union of collaboration with the United States in bringing about Chinese encirclement.[1]

The polycentric tendencies of recent years are no sure indication that bipolarity has come to an end. The easing of tensions, the assertion of independence on the part of third states, and the greater liberality of transbloc relations all have come at a time when the nuclear stalemate seems to preclude a drastic relocation of the balance of power. However, the preponderance of the Big Two makes it appear doubtful, as has been argued in the preceding chapters, that such manifestations are expressions of genuine independence, capable of developing into an enduring polycentric situation. Even France and China would have to abide by an agreement for international cooperation between the United States and the Soviet Union.

At present, the war in Vietnam represents a major disturbance in American-Russian relations. Although the role of chief political and ideological antagonist of the United States has passed to China, the Soviet Union has not seen fit to remain aloof, despite the obvious advantages that it might derive from nonparticipation. In its moral and material support of North Vietnam, it has, very likely, been motivated more by the desire to limit Chinese power than American power. Evidently, the Soviet Union is not prepared to let Asia go to China by default. It will, therefore, be difficult to reach an enduring and definite understanding between the United States and the Soviet Union concerning the policing of the world until the struggle over Asia is settled.

The long-range outlook for the balance of power will depend largely on whether the United States and the Soviet Union will be able to agree on measures to prevent nuclear diffusion. There can be little doubt that nuclear proliferation would not be in the interest of either the superpowers or the world at large. The exclusive possession of first-rate nuclear establishments by the Big Two and the nuclear balance between them are the best insurance against all-out nuclear war. As the number of nuclear powers increases, so does the chance of nuclear war. Although it is unlikely in the foreseeable future that third nations, if they were to develop nuclear arms without restraint, would be able to handle an all-out nuclear war, they could acquire sufficient nuclear power to cause major destruction and to spark off a war between the United States and the Soviet Union.

The awareness of the dangers inherent in nuclear proliferation is widespread, and both the superpowers and third nations are giving much thought to the problem. The United States, in particular, has unremittingly and dramatically expressed its concern. Its efforts have culminated in an antiproliferation treaty with the Soviet Union. Even in the absence of a treaty, the United States had taken measures to minimize the possibility of nuclear diffusion. In working out plans for sharing nuclear arms with its allies, the United States has insisted on retaining ultimate control. Its refusal to help France develop its own atomic weapons has been a major source of contention between the two nations; and since France has been slipping from American control, the United States has discontinued deliveries of enriched uranium fuel, essential to France's nuclear development.[2] When the United States has sold atomic reactors and fuels to other nations, it has tried to obtain the buyer nation's consent to inspection of its atomic installations to make sure that the installations are not diverted to military purposes. It has, furthermore, pressed for an international agreement to make inspection obligatory for other nuclear powers.

The enforcement of the international arrangement to prevent nuclear proliferation, to be sure, will be inordinately difficult. Moreover, there remains little time to work out appropriate measures. The further proliferation advances, the harder it will be to curb it. The United States and the Soviet Union have the physical power to prevent nuclear diffusion: by exerting pressures of a military, political, and economic nature; by giving guarantees to those in need of protection; and by providing inducements. The task is rendered difficult by the continuation of the cold war. The Big Two will remain absorbed in efforts to outmaneuver each other. For that reason, they will not risk losing favor with allies and uncommitted states. Their effort to acquire and maintain maximum support will constitute a strong temptation to remain inactive while other nuclear powers emerge. Moreover, the effectiveness of the arrangement will depend on the willingness of the superpowers to submit to restrictions on their own nuclear development.

The major difficulty with treaties of this nature is to make them palatable to third nations, and to ensure the latters' compliance. France and China have, thus far, refused to adhere to the test ban treaty, and the nuclear issue has caused restiveness among the United States' European allies. The problem, then, is largely political. The European allies presently depend on American nuclear power for their defense and will continue to do so for some time. They also know this military unilateralism implies political subordination to the United States. Thus, Great Britain and France have objected—largely as a matter of prestige—to inspection over atomic assistance for peaceful uses, and non-nuclear nations such as India and Israel—also for reasons of prestige—have been resentful of a dual standard of control, if similar safeguards are not applied to the nuclear powers.[3]

These difficulties should not obscure the fact that in some ways nuclear development is self-limiting. The exorbitant cost and the enormous resources—human and material—required to build and maintain a first-rate nuclear force exceed the capabilities of most nations. Moreover, the possession of such a force would impose burdensome international responsibilities upon the possessor, thus having little attraction for nations engaged in building up their societies and desiring more than anything else to be left alone. It is noteworthy that at the disarmament conference in the summer of 1965, the nonaligned nations were committed to neither side in the American-Soviet disagreement over a proposed nonproliferation treaty.[4] The desire of some third nations to avoid nuclearization has also been manifested by Mexico's proposal, supported by a number of other American states, to keep Latin America free of nuclear weapons.[5]

Enforcement difficulties, though considerable, do not appear insurmountable. Pressure could, no doubt, be effectively brought to bear, jointly by the superpowers, on any violator of an antiproliferation treaty. The more serious problem is the existing differences between the United States and the Soviet Union that are closely related to the politics of the cold war. And both fear the demoralizing effect on their allies of a nuclear agreement. Nevertheless, an encouraging sign of the increasing rationality of international politics in the bipolar world is that the area of agreement between the superpowers has been widened. There is a well-founded hope that the urgency of the nuclear problem will force the subordination of political conflicts to an extent that will make joint action possible before all is lost.

NOTES

CHAPTER ONE
BIPOLARITY: MYTH OR REALITY?

1 *The New York Times,* August 12, 1966, p. 8.
2 Secretary of State Dean Rusk spoke of the possible use of United States armed forces in "collective defense against armed aggression." *The New York Times,* August 26, 1966, p. 1.
3 *The New York Times,* August 27, 1966, p. 1.
4 Inis L. Claude, Jr., *Power and International Relations* (New York: Random House, 1962).
5 I have followed the analysis of the balance of power as a system in *ibid.,* p. 42.
6 *The New York Times,* June 21, 1966, p. 1.
7 *The New York Times,* July 31, 1966, p. 3 E.
8 *The New York Times,* June 27, 1966, p. 2.
9 *The New York Times,* July 9, 1966, p. 1.

CHAPTER TWO
THE ORIGINS OF CONTEMPORARY BIPOLARITY

1 Cordell Hull, *The Memoirs of Cordell Hull,* Vol. II (New York: Macmillan, 1948), p. 1639.
2 W. S. Churchill, *The Hinge of Fate* (Boston: Houghton Mifflin, 1950), p. 755.
3 Chester Wilmot, *The Struggle for Europe* (New York: Harper & Row, 1952), pp. 130, 636.
4 W. S. Churchill, *Triumph and Tragedy* (Boston: Houghton Mifflin, 1953), p. 65.
5 Wilmot, *op. cit.,* p. 447.
6 J. F. C. Fuller, *The Conduct of War, 1789–1961* (New Brunswick, N.J.: Rutgers University Press, 1961), pp. 264–266.
7 W. S. Churchill, *The Hinge of Fate,* pp. 689–691.

CHAPTER THREE
COLD WAR AND COEXISTENCE

1 President Eisenhower's foreign policy speech delivered in San Francisco, as quoted by *The New York Times,* October 9, 1952, p. 1.
2 *The New York Times,* November 28, 1957, p. 28.

3 George F. Kennan, "Disengagement Revisited," *Foreign Affairs,* XXXVII (1959), p. 188.

4 Quincy Wright, "Some Legal Aspects of the Berlin Crisis," *American Journal of International Law,* LV (January 1961), p. 960.

5 *The New York Times,* August 19, 1961, p. 2.

6 D. Healey, "The Crisis in Europe: A British View," *International Affairs,* XXXVIII (April 1962), pp. 145–155.

7 The Soviet understanding of the meaning of coexistence is stated for American audiences in Nikita Khrushchev, "On Peaceful Coexistence," *Foreign Affairs,* XXXVIII (October 1959), pp. 1–18.

8 *The New York Times,* September 2, 1966, p. 1.

9 *The New York Times,* September 9, 1966, p. 3.

10 Nikita Khrushchev, as quoted by *The Christian Science Monitor,* February 28, 1963, p. 1.

11 President Kennedy's address at the University of Maine, as quoted by *The New York Times,* October 20, 1963, p. 1.

12 *The Washington Post,* October 22, 1963, p. A 17.

CHAPTER FOUR
COLD WAR STRATEGY AND POLITICS

1 Nikita Khrushchev as quoted by Averell Harriman, *Peace with Russia?* (New York: Simon & Schuster, 1959), p. 167.

2 The mutual interest in maintaining the status quo comes out clearly in President Kennedy's address at The American University on June 10, 1963, quoted in *The New York Times,* June 11, 1963, p. 1.

3 S. de Madariaga, *The Blowing Up of the Parthenon or How to Lose the Cold War* (New York: Praeger, 1960), p. 83.

4 *The New York Times,* September 20, 1964, p. 1.

5 *The New York Times,* January 31, 1965, p. 1.

6 *The New York Times,* February 6, 1966, p. 1.

7 Benjamin Welles, "Soviet Drive Seen for Widened Ties," *The New York Times,* January 16, 1966, p. 10. James Reston, "Washington: The Tragedy of Skepticism," *The New York Times,* October 2, 1966, p. 10 E, reported that the recurrent peace proposals were not well received because the United States was not able to convince the world of its sincerity. The cool reception

demonstrates that peace offensives can boomerang if used in inappropriate circumstances. The desire of the Administration to appease domestic pressures at the same time that it is in possession of unchallengeable military power has created an atmosphere of suspicion that has deprived the peace offensive of all effectiveness.

8 See J. W. Spanier and J. L. Nogee, *The Politics of Disarmament: A Study of Soviet-American Gamesmanship* (New York: Praeger, 1962), Introduction.

9 *The New York Times,* August 18, 1965, p. 1.

10 Statement by Nikita Khrushchev, as reported by *The New York Times,* September 20, 1964, p. 8.

11 See C. L. Sulzberger, "Foreign Affairs: Moscow as an Asian Banker," *The New York Times,* October 24, 1965, p. 10 E.

12 J. M. Mackintosh, *Strategy and Tactics of Soviet Foreign Policy* (New York and London: Oxford University Press, 1963), p. 323.

13 *The New York Times,* August 21, 1965, p. 2.

14 The point is made by A. J. Toynbee, *America and the World Revolution* (London: Oxford University Press, 1962), *passim.*

15 President Kennedy, as quoted by *The New York Times,* March 14, 1961, p. 1.

16 U.S. President's Committee to Strengthen the Security of the Free World, *The Scope and Distribution of United States Military and Economic Assistance Programs* (Washington, D.C.: Government Printing Office, 1963).

17 Richard M. Nixon, as quoted by *The New York Times,* March 14, 1961, p. 1.

18 Alvin Shuster, *The New York Times,* June 25, 1961, p. E 3. Reportedly, the policy pronounced by Edward R. Murrow, then director of the USIA, has been of value in Africa, Latin America, Asia, and the Soviet Union in obtaining some understanding for the American Vietnam policy. It has been less successful in Western Europe and Japan. *The New York Times,* September 4, 1966, p. 2.

CHAPTER FIVE
THE SUPERPOWERS AND THEIR CLIENTELE

1 *The New York Times,* July 6, 1964, p. 1.

2 Statement of Under Secretary of State Christian Herter

before the Senate Committee on Foreign Relations on April 21, 1959, as cited by Dean Acheson, "The Practice of Partnership," *Foreign Affairs,* XLI (January 1963), p. 251.

3 Statement of Senate Foreign Relations Committee report on the Foreign Aid Bill, as quoted by *The New York Times,* July 8, 1966, p. 1.

4 *The New York Times,* October 2, 1966, p. 1.

5 Drew Middleton, "Realism About Rumania," *The New York Times,* July 31, 1964, p. 3.

6 The United States went far to avoid an open break, and at one time even abetted French efforts to build an independent nuclear force by granting permission to a French military plane en route to an atomic proving ground to land and refuel in possible contravention of obligations under the limited nuclear test ban treaty. *The New York Times,* December 6, 1964, p. 3.

7 *The New York Times,* November 21, 1965, p. 1 E.

8 *The New York Times,* March 27, 1966, p. 7.

9 *The New York Times,* August 2, 1965, p. 1.

10 *The New York Times,* January 24, 1965, p. 18; Richard Eder, "Johnson Affirms Latin Aid Pledge," *ibid.,* August 18, 1965, p. 1; Arthur J. Olsen, "Development Aid Is Pledged at Rio," *ibid.,* November 28, 1965, p. 1.

11 *The New York Times,* August 29, 1967, p. 3.

12 Robert Trumbull, "Now North Korea Talks Independence," in *The New York Times,* August 21, 1966, p. E 3.

13 *The New York Times,* September 10, 1966, p. 1.

14 *The New York Times,* July 9, 1966, p. 1.

15 "French Memorandum Delivered to the Governments of the Atlantic Alliance on March 8 and 10, 1966," *Ambassade de France—Service de Presse et d'Information,* French Affairs, No. 192.

16 *Ibid.*

17 *The New York Times,* April 24, 1966, p. 2 E.

18 *The New York Times,* July 8, 1966, p. 4.

19 *The New York Times,* January 6, 1966, p. 3.

20 Drew Middleton, "De Gaulle's Flirtation with Moscow," in *The New York Times,* April 4, 1965, p. E 3.

21 *The New York Times,* June 21, 1966, p. 1.

22 *The New York Times,* November 10, 1963, p. 1.

23 French Premier Georges Pompidou in an address to the National Assembly, as quoted by *The New York Times,* April 24, 1966, p. E 3.

24 *The New York Times*, August 25, 1966, p. 12.
25 *The New York Times*, August 20, 1966, p. 8.
26 *The New York Times*, August 7, 1966, p. 13.

CHAPTER SIX
THE NONALIGNED

1 UPI report of Secretary of State Dean Rusk's position given at a closed hearing of the House Foreign Affairs Committee, as cited in *Palo Alto Times*, July 4, 1962, p. 8.

2 Richard M. Nixon in an address to the American Society of Newspaper Editors, as quoted by *The New York Times*, April 21, 1963, p. 1.

3 *The Christian Science Monitor*, August 11, 1962, p. 16.

4 *The New York Times*, July 21, 1963, p. 1.

5 See Oskar Spett, "Der Erste Afrikanistenkongress in Accra," *Aussenpolitik*, Stuttgart (March 1963), p. 177.

6 *The New York Times*, December 8, 1963, p. 20.

7 Seymour Topping, "The 'Twilight' War in Laos," *The New York Times*, January 24, 1965, p. 4 E.

8 *The New York Times*, April 28, 1963, p. 3.

9 Sékou Touré, "Africa's Future and the World," *Foreign Affairs*, XLI (October 1962), p. 151.

10 *The New York Times*, June 16, 1963, p. 2 E.

11 *The New York Times*, November 22, 1963, p. 1.

12 The Asian nationalists are more pacifistic and anarchistic than communistic and seem to have little taste for total revolution. See Richard Harris, "Communism and Asia," *International Affairs*, XXXIX (January 1963), pp. 13–23.

13 *The Christian Science Monitor*, August 4, 1962, p. 1.

14 The United States has also refused to help Pakistan in the Kashmir dispute out of consideration for India.

15 Jawaharlal Nehru, as quoted by Sharokh Sabavala, *The Christian Science Monitor*, January 15, 1963, p. 2.

16 Seymour Topping, "Cambodia: Calm Land Under War Pressures," *The New York Times*, January 9, 1966, p. 6 E.

17 *The New York Times*, September 29, 1963, p. 15.

18 *The New York Times*, September 23, 1962, p. 23.

19 Habib Bourguiba, as quoted by *The New York Times*, July 25, 1961, p. 2.

20 It is not only the Big Two who have pointed to the pitfalls of neutrality. Recently the Australian Minister for

External Affairs dismissed the neutralization of Southeast Asia as an "impractical dream." He said, "We're in a world power struggle. You've got to stand up and be counted—you've got to say which side you're on. We know which side we're on and we're going to stick to that side." As quoted by *The New York Times*, June 15, 1964, p. 1.

21 See C. G. Rosberg, Jr. and A. Segal, *An East African Federation*, International Conciliation No. 543 (New York: Carnegie Endowment for International Peace, May 1963), *passim*.

22 Raymond Daniell, "Thant Says Continued Ignoring of U.N. Will End Power to Act," *The New York Times*, May 23, 1965, p. 1; Drew Middleton, "U.N. Assembly Ends with Little Achieved," *The New York Times*, December 26, 1965, p. E 3.

23 *The New York Times*, September 15, 1963, pp. 2, 3, E 11.

24 *The New York Times*, September 24, 1967, p. 4 E.

25 Drew Middleton, "Africans Talk and Talk About Africa," *The New York Times*, October 9, 1966, p. E 3.

26 Inis L. Claude, Jr., "The Management of Power in the Changing United Nations," *International Organization*, Vol. XV, No. 2 (1961), p. 235.

CHAPTER SEVEN
IDEOLOGY, POWER, AND LAW

1 B. D. Wolfe, "Communist Ideology and Soviet Foreign Policy," *Foreign Affairs*, XLI (October 1962), p. 157.

2 *The New York Times*, February 6, 1963, p. 1.

3 Editorial in the Communist Party newspaper *Jehmin Jih Pao*, as cited by *The New York Times*, July 14, 1963, p. 1.

4 Arthur Krock, "Kennedy's New Policies," *The New York Times*, June 16, 1963, Section IV, p. E 11.

5 A good example is the approval with only a narrow margin by the Israeli parliament of the withdrawal of troops from Suez previously agreed to by the government. Had the Knesset voted negatively, the United States would have found itself in a most embarrassing position.

6 *The New York Times*, April 28, 1963, p. 8.

7 *The New York Times*, March 20, 1963, p. 6.

8 Tad Szulc, "U.S. Aides Rebuff Castro on Peace Talk Overture," *The New York Times,* July 7, 1964, p. 1.

9 *The New York Times,* September 5, 1967, p. 1.

10 Expressions by various representatives of the United States government concerning Cuba point up the tenuousness of international law in the bipolar world. For example, Senator Capehart reportedly justified the possibility of occupying Cuba legally on the basis of the Monroe Doctrine (B. B. Johansson, "New Cuban Bid to Soviets," *The Christian Science Monitor,* August 28, 1962, p. 1). Such a broad interpretation of the right of self-defense would seem to imply that almost any change in Cuba, causing the displeasure of the United States, would justify American intervention, that is, all definable limits would disappear. Capehart's views, no doubt, are somewhat extreme. However, Adlai Stevenson's remarks in the United Nations on September 21, 1962, express similar sentiments: "While we will not commit aggression; we will take whatever steps are necessary to prevent the government of Cuba from seeking to subvert any part of this hemisphere." As quoted by *The New York Times,* September 22, 1962, p. 1. Nor does the Administration appear to have made any serious attempts to interfere with attacks on Cuba although, since the Bay of Pigs, it has been careful not to violate overtly the formal requirements of international law.

11 P. C. Jessup, "Should International Law Recognize an Intermediate Status between Peace and War?," *American Journal of International Law*, XLVIII (January, 1954), pp. 98–103.

12 Adlai Stevenson in a speech before the United Nations General Assembly, as quoted by *The Christian Science Monitor,* September 21, 1962, p. 1.

13 Annual report on the work of the United Nations during the year ended June 15, 1961, as quoted by *The New York Times,* August 25, 1961, p. 1.

14 John N. Hazard, "Co-Existence Codification Reconsidered," *American Journal of International Law*, LVII (January 1963), pp. 88–97.

15 See John N. Hazard, "Co-Existence Law Bows Out," *American Journal of International Law*, LIX (January 1965), p. 59.

16 For a fuller discussion of the American and Soviet posi-

tions, see John N. Hazard, "Co-Existence Codification Reconsidered," *op. cit., passim.* Also, E. McWhinney, " 'Peaceful Co-Existence' and Soviet-Western International Law," *American Journal of International Law,* LVI (October 1962), pp. 951–970.

17 E. McWhinney, *op. cit.,* pp. 955–957.

18 Professor G. I. Tunkin, quoted in *ibid.,* p. 962.

19 Carl Schmitt, *Völkerrechtliche Grossraumordnung* (Berlin, 1941), p. 43.

20 For an interesting discussion of the Monroe Doctrine, see Carl Schmitt, *Der Nomos der Erde im Völkerrecht des Jus Publicum Europaeum* (Köln: 1950), pp. 256–270.

21 See E. McWhinney, "Coexistence, The Cuba Crisis, and Cold War International Law," *International Journal,* XVIII (Winter 1962–1963), pp. 67–74.

22 *Ibid.,* p. 69. Even in criticizing the American action and paying lip service to the sanctity of international law, Khrushchev hinted at the need for reciprocity: ". . . you must admit that other countries have no lesser ground for acting in the same way with regard to the states on the territory of which preparations are really being made which constitute a threat to the security of the Soviet Union." Note to President Kennedy, as quoted by *The New York Times,* April 23, 1961, p. 25.

23 E. McWhinney, "Coexistence, the Cuba Crisis, and Cold War International Law," *op. cit.,* pp. 67–68.

24 *The New York Times,* April 19, 1964, p. 5.

25 Carl Schmitt, *Völkerrechtliche Grossraumordnung, passim.*

CHAPTER EIGHT
CONCLUSION

1 Seymour Topping, "New Phase of China-Soviet Rift Centers on U.S. Encirclement," *The New York Times,* February 6, 1966, p. 1.

2 *The New York Times,* April 17, 1966, p. 1.

3 John W. Finney, "Allies Resist U.S. on Atom Controls," *The New York Times,* January 16, 1966, p. 20.

4 *The New York Times,* August 5, 1965, p. 2.

5 *The New York Times,* April 17, 1966, p. 28.

BIBLIOGRAPHY

CHAPTER ONE
BIPOLARITY: MYTH OR REALITY?

Burton, J. W. *International Relations: A General Theory*. New York: Cambridge University Press, 1966.

Claude, I. L., Jr. *Power and International Relations*. New York: Random House, 1962.

Gulick, E. V. *Europe's Classical Balance of Power*. Ithaca, N.Y.: Cornell University Press, 1955.

Kaplan, M. A. *System and Process in International Politics*. New York: Wiley, 1957.

Liska, George. *International Equilibrium*. Cambridge, Mass.: Harvard University Press, 1957.

Morgenthau, H. J. *Politics Among Nations*. New York: Knopf, 1967.

————. *In Defense of the National Interest*. New York: Knopf, 1951.

Schwarzenberger, George. *Power Politics*. New York: Praeger, 1951.

Strausz-Hupé, Robert. *The Balance of Tomorrow*. New York: Putnam, 1945.

Wight, Martin. *Power Politics*. London: Royal Institute of International Affairs, 1946.

CHAPTER TWO
THE ORIGINS OF CONTEMPORARY BIPOLARITY

Churchill, W. S. *The Second World War*, 6 vols. Boston: Houghton Mifflin, 1948–1953.

Eisenhower, D. D. *Crusade in Europe*. Garden City, N.Y.: Doubleday, 1948.

Falls, C. B. *The Second World War*. London: Methuen, 1948.

Fuller, J. F. C. *The Second World War, 1939–1945*. London: Eyre & Spottiswoode, 1948.

Ismay, H. L. I. *Memoirs*. New York: Viking, 1960.

Kochan, Lionel. *The Struggle for Germany 1914–1945*. Edinburgh: University Press, 1963.

Sherwood, R. E. *Roosevelt and Hopkins*. New York: Harper & Row, 1948.

Stilwell, J. W. *The Stilwell Papers*. T. H. White, ed. New York: Sloane, 1948.

Wilmot, Chester. *The Struggle for Europe.* New York: Harper & Row, 1952

CHAPTER THREE
COLD WAR AND COEXISTENCE

Dulles, J. F. *War or Peace.* New York: Macmillan, 1950.

Ingram, Kenneth. *History of the Cold War.* London: Darwen Finlayson, 1955.

Kennedy, J. F. *The Strategy of Peace.* Allan Nevins, ed. New York: Harper & Row, 1960.

Lukacs, J. A. *A History of the Cold War.* Garden City, N.Y.: Doubleday, 1961.

Mager, N. H. and Jacques Katel. *Conquest without War.* New York: Simon and Schuster, 1961.

Madariaga, Salvador de. *The Blowing Up of the Parthenon, or How to Lose the Cold War.* New York: Praeger, 1960.

Malik, Charles. *Man in the Struggle for Peace.* New York: Harper & Row, 1963.

Overstreet, Harry, and Bonaro Overstreet. *The War Called Peace.* New York: Norton, 1961.

Seabury, Paul. *The Rise and Decline of the Cold War.* New York: Basic Books, 1967.

Slessor, Sir John. *What Price Coexistence.* New York: Praeger, 1961.

Seton-Watson, Hugh. *Neither War Nor Peace.* New York: Praeger, 1960.

CHAPTER FOUR
COLD WAR STRATEGY AND POLITICS

Beaton, Leonard, and John Maddox. *The Spread of Nuclear Weapons.* New York: Praeger, 1962.

Burton, J. W. *Peace Theory.* New York: Knopf, 1962.

Eisenhower, M. S. *The Wine Is Bitter.* New York: Doubleday, 1963.

Finletter, T. F. *Power and Policy.* New York: Harcourt, Brace & World, 1954.

Heilbroner, R. L. *The Future as History.* New York: Grove Press, 1961.

Horelick, A. L., and Myron Rush. *Strategic Power and Soviet Foreign Policy.* Chicago: University of Chicago Press, 1966.

Huntington, S. P., ed. *Changing Patterns of Military Politics.* New York: Free Press, 1962.

Kahn, Herman. *On Thermonuclear War*. Princeton, N.J.: Princeton University Press, 1960.

Kissinger, H. A. *Nuclear Weapons and Foreign Policy*. New York: Harper & Row, 1957.

Levine, R. A. *The Arms Debate*. Cambridge, Mass.: Harvard University Press, 1963.

Maritano, Nino, and A. H. Obaid. *An Alliance for Progress*. Minneapolis: Denison, 1963.

Montgomery, J. D. *The Politics of Foreign Aid*. New York: Praeger, 1962.

Schmitt, K. M., and D. D. Burks. *Evolution or Chaos*. New York: Praeger, 1963.

Spanier, J. W., and J. L. Nogee. *The Politics of Disarmament*. New York: Praeger, 1962.

Strausz-Hupé, Robert, W. R. Kintner, and S. T. Possony. *A Forward Strategy for America*. New York: Harper & Row, 1961.

Strausz-Hupé, Robert, W. R. Kintner, J. E. Dougherty, and A. J. Cottrell. *Protracted Conflict*. New York: Harper & Row, 1959.

Sulzberger, C. L. *What's Wrong with U.S. Foreign Policy*. New York: Harcourt, Brace & World, 1959.

Wadsworth, J. J. *The Price of Peace*. New York: Praeger, 1962.

Williams, W. A. *The Tragedy of American Diplomacy*. Cleveland: World Publishing, 1959.

CHAPTER FIVE
THE SUPERPOWERS AND THEIR CLIENTELE

Hoffman, G. W. and F. W. Neal. *Yugoslavia and the New Communism*. New York: Twentieth Century Fund, 1962.

Kalb, Marvin. *Dragon in the Kremlin*. New York: Dutton, 1961.

Laqueur, Walter, and Leopold Labedz, ed. *Polycentrism*. New York: Praeger, 1962.

Osgood, R. E. *NATO, The Entangling Alliance*. Chicago: University of Chicago Press, 1962.

Wolfers, Arnold, ed. *Alliance Policy in the Cold War*. Baltimore: Johns Hopkins University Press, 1959.

CHAPTER SIX
THE NONALIGNED

Brecher, Michael. *The New States of Asia*. London: Oxford University Press, 1963.

Dallin, Alexander. *The Soviet Union and the United Nations.* New York: Praeger, 1962.

Emerson, Rupert. *From Empire to Nation.* Cambridge, Mass.: Harvard University Press, 1960.

Gardner, R. N. *In Pursuit of World Order.* New York: Praeger, 1966.

Goodrich, L. M. *The United Nations.* New York: Crowell, 1959.

Kohn, Hans. *The Age of Nationalism.* New York: Harper & Row, 1962.

Lawson, Ruth, ed. *International Regional Organizations.* New York: Praeger, 1962.

Lyon, Peter. *Neutralism.* Leicester, England: Leicester University Press, 1963.

Martin, L. W., ed. *Neutralism and Nonalignment.* New York: Praeger, 1962.

Rossi, Mario. *The Third World.* New York: Funk & Wagnalls, 1963.

CHAPTER SEVEN
IDEOLOGY, POWER, AND LAW

Falk, R. A. *Law, Morality and War in the Contemporary World.* New York: Praeger, 1963.

Niebuhr, Reinhold. *Nations and Empires.* London: Faber & Faber, 1959.

———. *Christianity and Power Politics.* New York: Scribner, 1948.

———. *Moral Man and Immoral Society.* New York: Scribner, 1947.

Stone, Julius. *Aggression and World Order.* Berkeley: University of California Press, 1958.

Thompson, K. W. *Political Realism and the Crisis of World Politics.* Princeton, N.J.: Princeton University Press, 1960.

———. *Christian Ethics and the Dilemmas of Foreign Policy.* Durham, N.C.: Duke University Press, 1959.

Tucker, R. W. *The Just War.* Baltimore: Johns Hopkins University Press, 1960.